HEIR TO THE
CRESCENT
MOON

Iowa Prize for
Literary Nonfiction

HEIR TO THE CRESCENT MOON

Sufiya Abdur-Rahman

UNIVERSITY OF IOWA PRESS • IOWA CITY

University of Iowa Press, Iowa City 52242
Copyright © 2021 by Sufiya Abdur-Rahman
www.uipress.uiowa.edu
Printed in the United States of America

Cover design by Black Kat Design, LLC; text design by April Leidig

Printed on acid-free paper

Heir to the Crescent Moon is a work of nonfiction. Some names have been changed.
A portion of this book has appeared in slightly different form in *Ummah Wide*.

Library of Congress Cataloging-in-Publication Data
Names: Abdur-Rahman, Sufiya, author.
Title: Heir to the Crescent Moon / Sufiya Abdur-Rahman.
Description: Iowa City: University of Iowa Press, [2021] | Includes bibliographical
references. | "Winner of the Iowa Prize for Literary Nonfiction." |
Identifiers: LCCN 2021008764 (print) | LCCN 2021008765 (ebook) |
ISBN 9781609387839 (ebook) | ISBN 9781609387822 (paperback) |
ISBN 9781609387822 (paperback) | ISBN 9781609387839 (ebook)
Subjects: LCSH: Abdur-Rahman, Sufiya. | Muslims, black—United
States—Biography. | Muslim women—United States—Biography.
Classification: LCC BP62.B56 (ebook) | LCC BP62.B56 A234 2021 (print) |
DDC 297.092 [B]—dc23
LC record available at https://lccn.loc.gov/2021008764

To my siblings,
Idris, Aqil, Aliya, Isa, and Moe,
whose journeys inspired me
to explore my own

◆

I feel very strongly, though, that this amorphous people are in desperate search for something which will help them to re-establish their connection with themselves, and with one another. This can only begin to happen as the truth begins to be told.

—JAMES BALDWIN

CONTENTS

Prologue · My Father 1

PART I

1 · The Opening 7

2 · My Sister's Keeper 9

3 · Mercy (Ali vs. Liston) 13

4 · Black Muslim Ways 17

5 · Allah's Viceroy 21

6 · Seasons Change 25

7 · Found in Translation 29

8 · Snapping 33

9 · The Distance Between Us 41

PART II

10 · Made Whole 49

11 · Breathe Again 55

12 · Surrender at the Cinema 59

13 · The All American 67

14 · The Awakening (Mood Blue) 71

15 · Black Revolutionary 75

16 · Malcolm X Resurrects 79

17 · Becoming Muslim 87

PART III

18 · The ABCs 93

19 · Facing Destiny 97

20 · My Father Said So 101

21 · Long-Distance Mentality 109

22 · Club for Believers 115

23 · Thanksgiving 121

24 · America, the Beautiful 125

25 · Muslim, or Not? 131

26 · Her Own Way 141

27 · Better Muslim Than I 149

28 · Making Waves 153

29 · Islamic Sensibility 157

30 · What's in a Name? 159

31 · The Stars Align 163

32 · Meant to Be 169

33 · No Turning Back 175

34 · Dumb 179

35 · The Spirit of Allah 187

36 · My Burden 195

37 · Darkness on the Horizon 201

38 · We Wouldn't Be Here 207

39 · The Search for Truth 213

PART IV

40 · Being Black and Muslim 221

41 · Revelation 223

42 · My Fault 227

43 · All That Was Left 231

44 · Wishing Him Well 235

45 · History Holds Power 237

Epilogue · My Son 243

References 249

Acknowledgments 253

HEIR TO THE CRESCENT MOON

PROLOGUE

My Father

BEFORE I EVEN UNDERSTOOD what a Muslim was, I knew I wanted to be one. Because my father was. Both of my parents were. This meant that I was too. But simply *being born* Muslim was not enough. When I was five years old, in 1984, my father taught me that *being* Muslim is something more.

He had a way of gliding into a room, walking on the balls of his feet like his heels were too good to touch ground. His steps were soundless that day except for the faint swishing of his ashen soles across our cheap linoleum. I watched him as he strode from the hallway into the dining room, fingering a string of beads in his right hand. I had seen them before, hanging from a nail in the wall of his office at the opposite end of the hallway most of the time and clenched in his hand at others.

The beads were simple: plain brown, perfectly round, smaller than marbles but bigger than sweet peas. They were strung together like a necklace, except where the clasp should have been, one or two or three extra beads jutted out and led to a stiff brown tassel hanging from the end.

The flattened tips of my father's thumb and forefinger pinched each globe then inched along to the next, the string of beads rotating in his grasp like stairs on an escalator. He did this while walking—into the kitchen and over to the living room—with his fingers at my eye level, almost as if unaware of the movements they were making.

"What is that, Abi?" I asked my father, still eyeing the beads instead of looking at him. The little circles were plain but pretty and seemed like the kind of thing a girl like me should have. Dainty due to my size and fragile because of my timidity and penchant for bursting into tears if even looked at unkindly, I was often treated like a girly-girl—never mind that I hated dresses, dolls, the color pink, and any doubt that I could keep up with a boy my age. I thought if I asked nicely enough, my father might give the beads to me. He sat down in a chair faced backward from the dining room table and gathered me onto his lap. His caramel-complected face stared into mine, except his was framed by a low dark Afro behind his receding hairline and a full black beard shading his jaw and chin.

"These are dhikr beads. They're for praying," he said, still not holding them out for me to touch.

"But you're not praying," I said. "You're not even saying anything."

"I'm praying in my head," he explained. "You don't always have to pray out loud, but Allah should always be on your mind and in your heart." My father used the hand not holding the dhikr beads to point at my head and chest.

I knew by then that Allah was God. My father most often referred to Him as "the Creator." He created the sun, the moon, the stars, the land, and all the people on it. And for that, we worshipped Him.

My father uncurled his fingers to show me the beads laid lightly across his palm. It was here, in his hands, that I'd get lost in the intrigue that was my father. I'd grasp his fingers and stare at the back of his hand. It bulged with pulsating veins I pressed down on and watched jump from side to side to avoid my index finger's pressure. I'd turn his hand over and study his palm, the intricate conglomeration of lines, fingerprints, and creases so deep and dark they were like crevasses, dangerous erosions formed over time, through stress, and to be avoided at all costs—unless I could learn to read them, figure out what they meant. And so I held his hand at different angles, under varying lights, compared it to my grandfather's hand, and traced both of their creases with my tiny fingertips. Still, I couldn't decipher Abi. But I knew something was there.

With the dhikr beads obscuring his head line, life line, and fate line, my father explained there were two sets of thirty-three beads on the string and one of thirty-four, a set for each Arabic saying he would silently utter in remembrance of God—his prayer. The beads helped him keep count.

I realized then that my father would not be giving me the necklace. It was too important. I was still curious about it, though.

"How come we don't pray that way?" I asked, referring also to my ten-year-old sister and two brothers, eight and three. We prayed in Arabic but never with beads.

"You all don't have to do what I do," Abi said, his voice losing the levity it had taken on in talking to me, a child, and assuming its accustomed depth and deliberate diction. "Your mother and I are Muslim; we chose to be, but we're raising you all to be whatever you want."

It felt as though he were admonishing me. I didn't know what I'd done to deserve it, but my shoulders tensed and my back went stiff, as if sitting still would keep me from upsetting him further. Abi's tone told me that I was to take his words seriously, but I had a hard time understanding what they meant.

I knew that besides Muslims, there were Christians. Everyone in my extended family was Christian. Yet except for going over my grandparents' apartment on Christmas, where silver pine needles sporting multicolored metallic spheres jutted from a miniature tree atop a glass table—like some frozen relic from the ice-covered North Pole—we didn't do anything I thought could be considered Christian.

The only other religion I'd heard of then was Buddhism. And that was simply because of the mahogany brown, ceramic Buddha figurine the size of my stuffed hippo that sat perpetually plopped on an edge of the coffee table in my family's living room. My little brother and I sometimes rubbed its fat belly for good luck; we made no attempts to worship it. So I didn't see how my parents were raising us to be anything other than what I knew we were: Muslim.

Nevertheless, I listened as Abi continued: "When you're ready, that choice will be up to you. Understand?"

I nodded yes but didn't mean it. I only understood that I was what he was. And I would do what he did. He was my father, so I got my name from him, and my looks from him—according to all the relatives and friends who constantly reminded me—and I was to follow where he led.

The prospect of doing something contrary seemed nothing less than wrong.

And yet my father told each of my siblings and me the same thing: that it was his choice to be Muslim, but it didn't have to be ours. Over the years, he would come to rely on this refrain to avoid in-depth discussions of Islamic practices or detailed explanations of Muslim beliefs. He meant it to liberate us, to free us of the burden of being bound to a religion. But it didn't feel that way. "I'm Muslim," he'd say, his tone drenched and dripping in confidence, defiance, and pride, "but you all don't have to be," he'd add, dismissing us outright. Each time he said it, I wondered what Abi knew about Islam that he wasn't telling us. What hurt did he suffer in Islam that he thought, with a father's protection, we could avoid?

When Abi held my tiny torso within his hands, the string of prayer beads dangling by my side as he lowered me onto the floor, I felt certain that I knew what he was really trying to say, what he couldn't admit but secretly wanted. It was that I be what I felt I was supposed to be—was born to be: Muslim, just like him.

PART I

1

The Opening

THE HOUSE I GREW UP IN on Long Island's South Shore was my parents' last stop out of the Bronx, out of struggling to earn a living, on their way to building a comfortable middle-class existence for themselves and the family they had created together. The house's shingles were dark scarlet, like the blood my mother washed away when one of my siblings or I fought concrete for knee skin and lost; they were black cherry, like chunks in the vanilla ice cream my father scooped after another day spent dealing with white folks on his job. It had four bedrooms, two bathrooms, a garage, multicolored slabs of stone forming our back patio, thick vines of ivy climbing our rear fence, and a cherry and an apple tree blossoming in our front yard. A pair of windows poked from the second-story roof like widened eyeballs attuned to everything going on outside in our small Baldwin neighborhood. But inside was home.

My brothers, Muhammad and Isa, shared the room upstairs on the left. Across a tiny hallway, my big sister, Aliya, and I claimed our room on the right. My parents' bedroom was on the main level, but my father really spent most of his time in the room beside it, his office. Downstairs in the living room was where we all gathered before bedtime to pray.

"Aliya, Isa, Sufiya, Muhammad! Come downstairs," my father, in his booming bass, called us from oldest to youngest. And as though responding to a bolt of lightning, we all came running down the steps, consecutive claps of thunder. We plopped into various cross-legged positions atop couch cushions covered with midnight blue bedsheets, speckled white with images of twinkling stars. Each of us bowed our heads, closed our eyes, and, before our faces, parted and slightly cupped our hands as if poised to catch falling raindrops.

"*Bismillah al-rahman al-rahim. Alhamdulillahi rabbi-il al-amin. Al-rahman al-rahim . . .*"

I found such comfort in prayer. I prayed with my family every night back then. My ears would perk when our voices rose in unison, uttering a series of foreign words, some more challenging to pronounce than others.

"*Maliki yawmi din. Iyyaka na-buduwa, iyyaka nasta'iyn.*"

It was like singing a song, this prayer of ours. Abi led with a commanding baritone; my mother, Ummi, accompanied with a harmonic alto; Aliya, Isa, Muhammad, and I followed—poorly trained sopranos. Most of the tune was monotone, but in the places where the notes rose an octave or dipped to a depth I had to work to reach, the payoff was an audible beauty.

"*Ikhdinas siraa-til mustaqim.*"

I had no idea what the words meant. I never heard them spoken anywhere outside our own home. I only knew they were what we were supposed to say when praying to Allah. And I liked the sound of them, the way they rolled around in my mouth differently than the words I'd been saying all day, then slipped out and floated up like a ribbon of incense smoke into God's ear.

"*Siraa-til ikhdina 'an 'amta 'allayhim. Guyril makdubi 'allayhim. Walla-dau leen. Amin.*"

Instead of raindrops, I imagined Allah dropped His blessings into my open palms during the prayer. When it ended, I brought the edges of my hands together—careful not to let any gaps form between my fingers through which His grace could slip—and covered my nose, mouth, and eyes. Washing the blessing outward over my forehead, cheeks, and chin, I was cleansed. I opened my eyes to see my family around me, still drawn close.

2

My Sister's Keeper

MY SISTER HAD LEFT HOME. One afternoon when she was supposed to be there, probably watching us, her younger siblings, while our parents were out, she wasn't. Instead, as she'd told me she would, she'd run away. She couldn't stand living with my parents anymore. Although I knew that much, I didn't know why she couldn't. Or where she planned to go. Or how she planned to get there. Or what she'd do once she did.

So all the rest of us packed into my family's station wagon and drove around town looking for her. Though Aliya was the oldest and acted like it—bossing us around, refusing to play with Muhammad and me, talking back to Ummi and Abi—she was only ten. Ummi was frantic to find her before night fell.

While it was still light outside, Ummi worked the phone like a 411 operator: "Have you seen Aliya?" she'd asked all the parents of my sister's friends. But they hadn't. Once in the car, she became the backseat driver I never knew she could be. "Keep driving, Hassan. It's getting dark," she implored my father one minute, then barking, "Slow down! I can't see if she's out here," the next.

Eventually, I spotted Aliya walking down Grand Avenue, our town's main street, as if she had somewhere to go, more than a mile away from home. "She's over there," I alerted my parents.

"Where?" my mother asked.

"Over there," I pointed from the backseat to my petite sister wearing an Army surplus–style green jacket with a drawstring at the waist and a

9

long-strapped purse dangling from her shoulder. She was walking near the haunts of our town's homeless Vietnam vet, whom all the kids called Crazy Eddie—after the electronics store pitchman—with his wild hair, long beard, dirty skin, and alcohol breath. Abi pulled over beside her.

"Aliya, get in the car," he ordered.

She kept walking.

"Aliya," he raised his voice, and my sister slowed her gait, turned around, and approached the car.

Caught, her expression changed like the faces on a cedar totem, full of willful determination at first, then, with little space in between, the picture of painful resignation. She squished in beside my siblings and me before my father made a U-turn to take us home. Even though we were all glad to have found her, I knew right away that for Aliya there would be consequences.

That night, the fantasy I had of my father as Superman and Darth Vader all rolled into one loomed larger than the reality of the man before me. For that night, after rescuing a ten-year-old from the dangers of being alone, in the street, past dark, Abi commanded Aliya, Isa, me, and Muhammad to line up outside my bedroom door in that order. It turned out that the consequences would not be just for my sister but for all of us. We four stood in the tiny, crimson-carpeted vestibule, lit only by a single overhead bulb that cast shadows on everything and tinged even good memories with a hint of darkness.

But this was nothing good. We were each waiting our turn to be spanked. Abi called Aliya first. She was five years older than me, funny, outspoken, and seemingly not afraid of anything or anybody, but when the door opened for her to go in, her totem face changed from trepidation to terror. As if trying to enter undetected, she crept into our room, where we traded secrets after turning out our light at night and primped ourselves in the mirror above her dresser each morning before school. And from our room, I could hear her wailing after every thump of my father's thick-veined, flat-fingertipped hand.

"Don't you ever . . . ," Abi said in a worked-up high pitch, then he slammed his open palm—head line, life line, and fate line—down on what I knew was Aliya's bare behind. She let out a siren cry, more out of pain than of shame of wrongdoing. And I stood there listening, flinching, cringing—wishing I could be somewhere else.

But I couldn't leave. If my brothers and I weren't there when that bedroom door flung open, we would be in even bigger trouble than we were already. So I stayed put and tried to think of a way to avoid being beaten.

I could say that like everyone else, I didn't know where Aliya had gone. This was true, but unlike everyone else, I knew she was going to go and said nothing.

I could remind him that I'd helped find Aliya, I thought. It was my eagle eye that had spotted her first.

If that didn't work, I guessed my best defense against a spanking would be to point out that I wasn't even the one who'd fled. But that was my father's whole point. It didn't matter that Aliya was the one who had actually run away; we were all responsible, for not stopping her, for not telling him or our mother so they could intervene, for creating the conditions that made her want to leave her home in the first place, Abi said. We were a family, so we had to stick together and look out for each other. Abi wanted to teach us that we were each our sister's keeper. Because there was some doubt that my brothers and I, being so young, could mentally grasp that concept, my father had lined us up, ready to make sure each of our butts got the message.

The bedroom door parted, and Abi summoned Isa inside. Through the opening I could see Aliya hunched over a stool, her face scrunched in pain and eyes spewing tears like a broken faucet. As soon as Isa was in, Abi shut the door behind him.

I still couldn't believe he was serious. Who ever heard of punishing kids who hadn't really done anything wrong? Besides, Abi wouldn't actually hit Muhammad, would he? My little brother was only three; he wouldn't understand. Maybe it was all for show, I thought, and the spanking wouldn't even hurt. Either way, there would be no way out of it.

"Sufiya!" A shiver went through me when Abi bellowed from inside my room. It was my turn. Isa came walking out with tears streaming down his tough little face. If my big brother—my protector—was crying, I thought, there was no hope for me. I practically tip-toed toward my father, unable to explain why I didn't deserve to get spanked—why I hadn't been my sister's keeper. Before I was able to get any words out at all, he said, "Pull down your pants."

I soon found out that the thrashing was in no way simply symbolic. Even before feeling it, though, I realized that knowledge of the pain I'd inflicted on my family by keeping my sister's plan a secret—and that my father was in turn inflicting on me—was its own punishment. I did not yet understand why teaching us unity was so crucial for Abi. Nonetheless, the lesson made me cry.

3

Mercy
(Ali vs. Liston)

ABI WAS IN HIS OFFICE with the door closed. He'd been in there a long time. Whatever he was doing was important—at least that's what my siblings and I were made to feel.

"Don't disturb your father," Ummi told us. "Go on and play, but do it quietly."

Of course, my brothers, sister, and I proceeded to run wild through the whole house, stacking then demolishing our geometrically shaped wooden blocks in the basement; giggling while chasing each other through the hallways, living room, and up and down the stairs; playing the radio and breakdancing on my brothers' bedroom floor. The only time we attempted to stay quiet, in fact, was when we tiptoed past Abi's darkened doorway to Ummi's room beside it to tell on each other for one reason or another.

Abi's door remained shut. But his despair, his total and utter dejection, hung in the air beyond it. Like a specter present everywhere and nowhere at once, a profound sense of disappointment permeated the house, haunting each room with melancholy and ire even as we laughed and played.

I could not see beyond the door and walls in which he enclosed himself, but my father was before me nonetheless. In my illusion, he sat at his desk, back turned, face in hands, intermittently rubbing his head or beard, trying to suss out how and where he went wrong.

It seemed that just weeks or maybe months before, he was so happy. One bright weekend day, he'd packed us into the station wagon and driven Ummi and all of us kids into the city. We picked up Idris and Aqil, my oldest brothers, from their mother's apartment and searched for a newspaper stand or box selling Abi's latest venture, a magazine he called the *Caramel Apple*. He came up with the name because the magazine focused on arts and entertainment news in New York City, the Big Apple, for black readers, the caramel complected. (He found the name particularly clever.) That first publication day, it was enough of a thrill for Abi just to see the thing on sale. He beamed like the sun on a cloudless beach as he handed each of us six kids a trucker's cap emblazoned with the *Caramel Apple* logo and had us stand against a building in height order for pictures.

"Say *Caramel Apple*," he said, his thick lips spread into a wide grin.

"*Caramel Apple!*" we all grinned back.

To get that first issue ready, he'd held editorial meetings in our house. His and my mother's friends came over offering my siblings and me warm "as-salaamu'alaikums" before Abi assigned them all tasks and deadlines for their articles, interviews, and illustrations. Over the phone, he recruited his father, a foodie before there was such a thing, and my mother's mother, who seemed to bake preternaturally, to contribute recipes. After work and on weekends, he sat before his typewriter crafting letters onto *Caramel Apple* letterhead, trying to secure advertising and drum up publicity for the magazine. As production neared, Abi enlisted my siblings and me to help scour grocery stores for perfectly dipped caramel apples that we'd hold up while flashing him our sweetest smiles for promotional photos. He'd gotten everyone involved.

And then, after publishing only two issues, the *Caramel Apple* folded.

Abi's smile faded. His office door shut.

It opened once, and late at night I heard him and Ummi arguing about the magazine, their voices sharp with anger. If she had given him more support, he said, the magazine could have—or did he say *he* could have?—succeeded.

"I have given you everything you ever asked for, Hassan," my mother answered.

At one point, Abi taught me that the word Islam means "submission, submission to the will of Allah." To be a Muslim means to be "one who submits or surrenders to Allah's will." It sounded like a noble goal, to understand Allah well enough to know His will—and have the wherewithal to follow it. If only I could get to that point, I thought, all would be right. If it meant helping Allah achieve His aims, and I had some small part to play in that, I would gladly surrender myself.

I wondered then how much being a Muslim wife had to do with surrender. What part of helping the marriage achieve its aims depended on the wife's submitting to the will of her husband, not God, but clearly some kind of ruler?

Later, Abi's office door opened another time, and I heard my mother's voice cut the air with an awful, agonizing shriek.

My sister ran toward it, and I ran down the stairs after her. The scream came from the dining room. When I got there, what I saw transfixed me.

"Hassan! Hassan, no! Stop!" my mother shouted. She was splayed on her back on our brown linoleum floor, crying and screaming at my father, who acted as if he couldn't hear. Instead, he stood over her, his chest heaving up and down, a foot penning each of her hips. My mother's legs were folded onto themselves, arms reaching for both help and protection, fingers extended like electrified hair, face wet with tears, voice quaking with fear. And my father's stance, completely silent and perfectly still but poised to pounce, kept her there.

I was terrified into immobility. I wanted to—I felt I needed to—but knew I could not stop my father, and I dare not help my mother.

But how did she get down there, I wondered, conquered and vulnerable like Liston to my father's Ali? Did he hit her? Push her down? Drag her across the floor? All three? I didn't see. She was in a position of surrender, but she refused to surrender, would not submit. No, she was trying to get away, desperately calling his name while pleading for mercy as if to rouse him from a spell.

"Hassan! Hassan! Look at the children! You gonna do this in front of our children?"

Do what? I wondered. *Do what to my mother?*

Did my mother's "do this" mean beat her? Abi spanked us when we did something he thought was wrong. Would he do the same to Ummi? Had he already? The "do this" felt familiar, like she was well aware of what was coming and just had to think of something—anything—to stop it.

But my father had her trapped. He hadn't let her move since I got there.

I was trapped too, my feet seemingly stuck to the floor, my face frozen with fright.

"Hassan! Hassan! Look at them!"

And then he turned. With glassy yellow eyes, hunched shoulders, and heavy hands, he saw me and my siblings staring at him, wondering what, in God's name, was going on.

The spell broken, he staggered off, and we rushed to Ummi to help her up. Her weight in that moment was more than I expected, more than I could bear. But once she got to her feet, Ummi quickly and temporarily ushered us out of the house and away from danger, away from our father.

Afterward, no one would mention what happened that day. Even I, within a matter of days, would forget the incident completely. It became like a message written with an invisible marker; the memory—like the marker's strokes—vanished, no longer accessible in normal light. There, but not there. It was gone until my subconscious, years later, made the image of my mother on her back and my father seemingly daring her to get up—to stand up to him—occasionally, in quiet moments and darkened light, return to mind.

More than Abi's menacing presence, Ummi's powerlessness in that moment—and, in fact, in their marriage—frightened me. From her prone position on the ground, she could not protect us; she could not protect herself. We were all at the mercy of Abi's wrath.

4

Black Muslim Ways

THE SOUND OF THE PHONE ringing in our house was like a mechanized way to shout "Ummi" because the call was always for her.

"Hello," Ummi answered in her cheery singsong. "Wa'alaikum as-salaam, sis." That's all my siblings or I needed to hear to know it was either Umti Haniya, Umti Khadija, or Umti Zainab, my mother's three best Muslim friends, on the other end. We promptly rolled our eyes because we also knew we would immediately become ghosts to her—presences she could feel but seemed unable to see or hear except in an effort to dispel us—for at least a couple of hours, about how long each conversation lasted.

She took our 1970s-era dirty-blond handset from the wall, nestled it between her ear and shoulder, and snaked the spiral cord from where it originated at the edge of our dining room, down to her bedroom on the opposite end of the hallway. She attempted to close her bedroom door for privacy but there was no point; even with the door closed, Ummi spoke with such animation that we had no trouble hearing every word she said.

After exchanging salaams, their conversations usually moved to a well-check of the kids. If it was Umti Khadija, whose voice was as sweet as a stalk of fresh sugarcane and who usually called on weekends maybe every other week, Ummi would ask about Khalil, Ibrahim, Najwa, Shahid, and Muntaqima. Umti Khadija, like a couple of my mother's other Muslim friends, was one of the few people we knew with more kids in her family than we had in ours.

If it was Umti Haniya, whose voice was as bright as a field of sunflowers and who, because she called every weekend, my sister gave the nickname "Weekly," I might get confused while listening in. She had a son named Mohamed and whenever Ummi talked about him, I always thought she was talking about my brother Muhammad.

In fact, Umti Haniya's Mohamed was the only other Muhammad I knew, and my mother's friends and their children were the only other Muslims I knew. I didn't go to school with any; I didn't regularly come across any in my neighborhood park; my father didn't have many friends of his own. It was through my mother's frequent phone conversations with her sisterhood and the occasional visits they made to our house, or we to theirs, that I gained a working knowledge of at least some black Muslim ways. A common conversation, for example, proceeded like this: "Oh, Isa's doing well, alhamdulillah," Ummi might say. "He made three touchdowns in his football game last weekend. . . . And Sufiya? Yes, still carrying that hippo around. But she's about to lose another tooth, insha'Allah," she might add.

Listening in was how I acquired a basic Arabic vocabulary: *alhamdulillah* meant "praise God" or "thank God"; *insha'Allah* meant "God willing" or "hopefully"; *as-salaamu'alaikum* and *wa'alaikum as-salaam* were like saying hello, of course, but literally meant "peace be unto you" and "unto you, peace." With no regular trips to a mosque and no formal Qur'anic study, I had a lot to figure out on my own. And I had no community but the legend of boroughs-away kids my age, their khimar-wearing mothers, and my siblings who created elaborate jokes about it all, but who at least understood it.

After a while on the phone, Ummi engrossed herself in whatever drama her sister-friends were sharing that day or whatever story she found fit to tell them. When those conversations really got going, all I heard from her was a series of "guurrlls," giggles, and "astaghfirullahs," which came out so fast that for the longest time, I thought my mother was saying "stafallah." Stafallah meant that whatever she was laughing at, she knew wasn't really funny. Stafallah meant that whatever bit of gossip she was spreading, she knew she really shouldn't. Stafallah meant that whatever misfortune happened to the person she and her friend were talking about, it truly was a shame. And she was calling on Allah to have mercy on them for laughing and for spreading gossip, and she was calling for Allah's mercy on the sufferer of the misfortune. Astaghfirullah seemed to be a cure-all for minor un-Muslim-like infractions.

If the phone rang and it was Sister Zainab, as she called herself, whose voice dragged like a car being pulled by a tow truck and who called so often that my sister gave her the nickname "Daily," Ummi would ask about her daughter and her son, and there the conversation would stay. Her son, the first born, got into so much trouble. Her son caused his mother so much grief. His father was not always around, and that was more reason why her son could not seem to get himself together. And he was just a boy, maybe only a year or two older than me. Daily worried that the future didn't bode well for her son, so many of her conversations with my mother turned into makeshift therapy sessions: She talked, Ummi listened, and sometimes Ummi threw in her patented cheerful aphorisms to help pull her friend out of despair.

One weekend—in a rare occurrence—Sister Zainab brought her two kids from their apartment in the Bronx to visit us at our home in Long Island. Coming out to Long Island was a bit of a trek for them, but it mimicked the journey we took to get there. My parents, Aliya, and Isa used to live in the same apartment complex—Parkchester—as Zainab did before I was born. Then my family moved to LeFrak City in Queens, where I was born, and finally, we left the city altogether for Long Island. In Long Island, we lived in a house, had our own yard, and our father lived with us. That seemed to be the differentiating factor between our family and the families of the umtis: None of them had stable marriages or their children's father in the household. I never asked but was always curious about how each of the women felt about submission. With their covered heads but my mother's free-flowing hair, I assumed that their surrendering to God's will didn't seem to be a problem—which may have explained a difficulty with their surrender to a man.

If anybody had a problem with it, I figured it had to be Zainab. She was shorter than Ummi, who was just short enough to still shop in the petites section, rounder, and had perfect ebony skin that she passed on to both her kids. She may have covered her hair, but the style was more kerchief than khimar. And she was no nonsense. She didn't take much time for niceties with us children. Her guiding light at all times seemed to be discipline: making sure her kids abided by it and if not, demanding that they start. Her personality seemed to be so opposite my mother's that besides a common background in Islam and a couple of kids who were close in age, I couldn't tell what held their friendship together.

"As-salaamu'alaikum, Hassan," Zainab said as she walked into the house and past my father, greeting him with her customary slow mono-tone drawl and not bothering to conjure a smile. Then she dropped her son off with Isa and Muhammad, her daughter off with Aliya and me, and disappeared with Ummi into her bedroom. Inevitably, before long her son misbehaved. I didn't know how but it was enough to make his mother pull him into Ummi's bedroom, close the door behind him, and proceed to shout at him, her monotone rising and falling with anger and frustration. Then she opened the door, giving us the impression that the admonishment was over.

Instead, as plainly as if she were asking to borrow a cup of sugar, she said, "Labiba, do you have a belt I can use?" Ummi slipped into her room, rummaged through her closet, and handed her one. "No, Labiba. I need a thicker one," Zainab said, reverting to her tow-truck tone, low and weary as though she bore the weight of her son's success and very survival on her back, as she returned it. Ummi then went again to the closet and pulled out the thickest belt she owned—the only one her friend would accept—a wide white leather one with a big buckle and many holes, meant to be worn over a shirt and around the waist for style, not function.

"Thank you," Sister Zainab said, disappearing back into the room. The sound of her voice, her son's cries, and the smacks of leather against his body were all that escaped. My siblings and I took to calling the white belt "the notorious" because it was so big and so bad and what Zainab used to spank her first-born son with each time he came over.

5

Allah's Viceroy

IN FOURTH GRADE, a new girl arrived in my class. She had skin the color of a wet sand pit, big amber eyes, and dusty brown hair she wore in three or four elastic-tied sections of twists she stuffed with raggedy extensions. She ran fast; among the kids our age, she and I often traded the title of "fastest," depending on which of us had won the most recent race down her block or mine.

This new girl was popular, but picky about who could be her friend. Of the three other black girls in our grade, one was the color of roasted coffee beans and thus too dark-skinned to be this girl's friend. Another had hips the width of two of us put together and so was too fat to be this girl's friend. The third had severely bucked teeth and just wasn't cute enough to be this girl's friend. That left me. The new girl and I were about the same complexion in winter months, we both had bony knees and elbows, and my overbite was slight enough not to bother. Our alliterative first names also blended into a pleasant singsong reminiscent of poetry whenever spoken. Despite the fact that I didn't really like the new girl, she and I became close.

One morning, the new girl, the bucked-tooth girl, and I lingered in the back of Mrs. Vecchione's classroom hanging our coats up in the cubbies, or at least pretending to. The two girls came from devout Christian families and were discussing something about God. Suddenly, the new girl whipped around and told me, "You don't pray to the real God," as if answering a question I'd just asked.

"Yes I do," I snapped.

"No you don't. The Moozlum god is not the real God." By then, most of my classmates had learned my family was Muslim. With a name like Abdur-Rahman, always first when attendance was called, always requiring me to correct or assist the teacher's pronunciation, it brought questions.

"Yes, He is. It's the same God, just a different name," I explained.

"No, God is the only God."

She was agreeing with me. She just didn't know she was. Abi had taught me the main tenet of being Muslim was belief in one God: There is no god but Allah.

I told her, "Yeah, Allah is the Arabic word for God," thinking she'd finally understand.

The new girl, my supposed best friend, brought her face close to mine. "No. Your God, isn't real," she said rolling her neck, her breath smelling of the bubble gum she constantly popped. "And you're *not* gonna go to Heaven." She backed up. "You can ask my dad."

Her father was some sort of deacon or minister with a storefront congregation on our town's main street. This meant nothing to me, though, because in my ten-year-old's view, my dad was the foremost authority on Islam and could run circles around whatever religious teachings her dad thought he knew.

My dad had taught me and my siblings to pray in a different language, after all. And my dad had a Qur'an so huge, he had to have been an expert to read it. (It was big and blue with page edges that blended the colors of sun and rain, like a marbleized vision of the heavens from earth.) My dad could read from this Qur'an in both English and Arabic. And, according to what he told me, when my dad was "in the mosque," as he called it, the imam asked him to stand in at events when the imam himself couldn't go. I could ask my dad anything about Allah or Islam and he knew the answer—he wouldn't always tell me the answer, but I was sure he knew.

Yet there was no chance to even bring my dad into it. Class had already begun; the buck-toothed girl had taken her seat long before, while the new girl and I stood in the back arguing in a whisper. Then she walked away too, confident that in our spiritual dispute, she was the victor.

For a few moments, I stood there, apart from the class and my supposed best friend, unable to comprehend how anyone could see a resemblance between us. If she was a reflection of me in look, name, and ability, then she was the distortion I'd see in a funhouse mirror, deformed and grotesque. With her gone, I allowed the wall that separated the lacquered blond wood cubbies from the rest of the room to shield me as I wept. My tears weren't out of sadness but frustration, frustration that I'd failed to adequately defend my faith, and disappointment that I'd let Allah down.

"And you're not gonna go to heaven" echoed in my head as the familiar paralysis that gripped my vocal cords whenever I cried took over. But there was no longer anyone for my teacher to call to speak for me when I became too upset to do it for myself; Aliya and Isa had already graduated and Muhammad was just in second grade. Besides my little brother, I was the only Muslim in my school, Allah's sole viceroy. And now, because I flubbed my defense of Islam, the new girl would walk around, ruling her reluctant subjects as she did, thinking that being Muslim was an automatic condemnation to Hell.

How could you let that happen? I asked myself.

After several moments of sniffling amid otherwise perfect stillness, I wiped the wetness from my face and tried to brush defeat from my demeanor. Straightening my clothes, I shaped my lips into a half smile. I would not let the new girl know she had got the better of me. I would not let her see me cry. With undoubtedly moist eyes but my chin up, I emerged from the classroom's hideaway, alone—totally alone—and took my seat.

6

Seasons Change

ONE AFTERNOON THAT SPRING, as the cherry tree in our yard began to blossom in ripples of white and the breeze blew crisp and cool around my newly uncovered ears, my little brother and I were about halfway through our walk home from school when we spotted our mother's car parked at a corner. Her sky blue seven-seat hatchback sat on one side of Grand Avenue, facing home, while we bounced as if on pogo sticks watching it from the other side of the street.

Muhammad and I walked to and from school every day. Our route was slightly too short for us to be assigned a school bus but a little too long to be enjoyable; getting a ride any part of the way was a gift we were grateful to receive. Anxious for the ride but mindful of the crossing guard, we revved our engines at the crosswalk until the light turned green. Then, as it changed, Muhammad's and my legs kicked into gear, cutting through the air and racing past stopped traffic to see who could reach the car first. We barely slowed as we approached, but eased up enough to notice Aliya and Isa already in the back seats.

All right, I thought, *time for a family outing!*

Maybe we would go to Eisenhower Park, I hoped, to run around in its wide-open fields after being cooped up in school all day or out to eat, all of us together, at a restaurant. Getting to the car first, I pulled open a door and realized it was too early for dinner. As I climbed inside, the mood told me we wouldn't be going to a park either.

Isa was sitting in the middle row, stiff as concrete, his arms folded tightly over his chest. He didn't acknowledge Muhammad or me as we sat down. Aliya was sitting in the back row, whimpering. She sniffled, then gasped intermittently, her eyes red with tears. As I pushed over beside her, she pulled me close in an embrace that tightened as her sobs amplified, ringing in my ears. Frightened, I turned to Ummi.

She swiveled backward in the driver's seat to face us. And she looked normal—her shoulder-length hair pulled into a ponytail at the nape of her neck; a pair of red-framed sunglasses shaped like cat eyes perched atop her head; her skin warm like baked bread. The only difference was her smile. Beaming with kindness and an amusement with life, her toothy grin usually pushed ample cheeks skyward, crinkled her nose, and turned her eyes into little black pearls. She smiled and friends felt welcome, smiled and gift givers knew they were appreciated, smiled and strangers, too, became friends. But she didn't show that smile. Instead, she pursed her lips, revealing their raisin-like wrinkliness, and flashed only a few straight teeth. I could take no comfort in that grimace. Then Ummi spoke.

"Kids, your father and I are getting divorced."

She didn't bother to preface the news or couch it in a lot of flowery talk about love and family. She just ripped the Band-Aid off, unceremoniously and quickly, laying bare our raw emotions with no preparation to help us deal with them.

Aliya, who had released me from her embrace, sobbed louder, and when I looked over, I swore I saw a tear trickling down Isa's face in silence. I knew I was also supposed to be upset to the point of crying, that everyone was expecting me—who wept if I got a bad grade in school—to break down. Yet my eyes were dry. The news didn't surprise me. How could it? Ummi and Abi fought; I had never seen them affectionate with each other; and for years, they hadn't even shared the same bedroom. Ummi slept in the queen-sized bed in her bedroom. Abi slept next door atop a sturdy piece of plywood he'd installed just far enough from the ceiling of his office to lie down on, his loft. Aliya and Isa couldn't have been shocked by Ummi's news. What was bothering them so much then, I wondered. My mind flitted to what would happen to us kids if our parents divorced.

We would be separated. Split up as I had seen in so many TV movies and after-school specials. A judge would force two of us to go live with Ummi and the other two with Abi. There was always a custody battle in divorce, and the court would have to break us up because—based on what I saw on TV—four kids were too many for one person to raise alone. But which two would go where?

Aliya and Isa must be going with Abi, I thought; *that's why she hugged me so hard.* They were fifteen and thirteen and could handle living with a man who didn't cook much and never cleaned. Muhammad and I would stay with Ummi because we were eight and ten and still dependent on our mother. Or maybe Isa and Muhammad would stay with Abi because they were boys and needed to be raised by a man. And Aliya and I would live with Ummi.

Whichever way we were separated, I would have to be apart from someone I loved: either my big sister, who was teaching me how to dress, wear my hair, and speak up for myself, or my little brother, my partner in mischief and adventure. I couldn't stand the thought of either.

Only then did tears well up in my eyes so completely that it seemed as though everything in view had been soaked with rain. As my mind fast-forwarded to the broken home and broken family sure to be the end product of my mother's announcement, the wells of water gushed over my eyelids and onto my face. I didn't bother to wipe them away; only more would come. Feeling suddenly unmoored within the car, I wrapped my arms across my chest, holding myself in place, and Aliya again secured her arm around my shoulder.

Through my flowing tears, I watched my mother pull her red cat-eye shades out of her hair and place them over her eyes. They reminded me that at age thirty-four, Ummi was one of the youngest and prettiest among the moms of all my friends. And she would soon be a single mother. It didn't seem fair.

She turned around in her seat and steered the car into a U-turn. Wind rushed in from her open window, reminding me of the changing seasons. And I cursed the spring air that had no right to smell like jubilation at that moment. I damned the warm breeze blowing promise so inappropriately onto my tear-soaked face. My mother, alone in the front seat, began driving in the opposite direction of home.

7

Found in Translation

WHILE MY FAMILY WAS still living together but my parents were in the process of divorcing, having Abi teach me about Islam suddenly took precedence. Although I knew both Abi and Ummi had chosen to become Muslim as teens—independently of each other—Abi was the one I saw retreat to his loft to read the Qur'an; the one who'd tacked up in his office sepia-toned photos of Malcolm X and Sufi scholar Hazrat Inayat Khan; the one who led us in prayer. And that other, more foreboding image of Abi remained veiled in invisible ink.

Worried that I'd be forced to move away from my father before I got the chance to truly glean from his knowledge of Islam, one afternoon I approached him in his office: "Abi? Can you teach me what the prayer means?"

I was eleven years old and in fifth grade. No longer was I forced to sit on a metal stool beside the kitchen stove and watch as my mother turned a straightening comb into a weapon that backed down my willful mane and attacked my eavesdropping ears with singes and burns. Now I wore my permed hair in styles I created myself. Although hesitant to do so at first, I eventually accepted this hairstyling graduation as a rite of passage. Questioning my father in this way was one too.

"What do you mean?" he asked me from behind the glass-covered piece of wood he'd fashioned into a desk, piled with paper and envelopes of mail. Beneath the glass he'd slipped photographs: my siblings and me grinning beside his mother, his brother in cap and gown graduating from college, and other smile-filled moments of his family gazing up at him only when the desk was clear of his preoccupations.

"I mean in English. I know the Arabic words, but I want to know what they mean in English."

My family had begun praying again. We hadn't done so with any regularity for a few years. I realize now that returning to prayer must have been one of my father's failed attempts at keeping his family together.

"Why?" he asked, and I remembered that, when he wanted to, Abi could force a lesson out of every situation, mistake, or happenstance. When he came home from working in the city, he'd sometimes be carrying a new puzzle or game he found at the table of some street corner vendor or in the aisles of a specialty toy store. He bought us various Rubik's Cubes, a Black History Trivia board game, a mess of curved plastic tubes twisted into a ball we were supposed to unwind, and several other brain games. He would plop them on a coffee table and leave them for us to figure out. If weeks went by and an orange square on our cube remained surrounded by otherwise pristine green—to me a testament of our hard work and progress—Abi would walk by and remark, "Still haven't figured it out, huh?" For him, even when we played, we were supposed to be learning something.

"Um, because it's important," I said. "If I'm praying to Allah, I want to understand what I'm saying to Him."

Abi leaned back in his chair and, with a smirk, said "Oh," as if amused to have been set straight by a preteen. "All right. Go on upstairs and I'll be up there in a little while."

The sound of his deliberate footsteps on our creaky staircase was usually reason enough for my siblings and me to quickly pretend to be doing something useful, like homework or straightening up. That, accompanied by the frequent rumble of my father clearing his throat, which reminded me of a bowling ball barreling down a long, unlacquered lane, signaled he meant business. When I heard the creaks and rumble approaching this time, though, I just waited for the lesson I had requested.

Abi sat down on a stool in the room I still shared with Aliya and faced me. His broad shoulders and sober demeanor were slightly out of place against the backdrop of my room's carefree powder blue walls. But I had asked him to help and there he was. Instead of simply jotting the prayer down for me or handing me his Qur'an so I could read the English translation myself, he started by asking me what I remembered of the prayer.

"Bismillah," I began, which I already knew meant, "In the name of Allah." We said that to start the blessing before every meal.

"Al-rahman, al-rahim," I recited the next part. I thought that line's meaning would be easy to figure out since it contained part of our last name, Abdur-Rahman. For years, I had been telling people with pride that it meant "servant of the Most High" or "servant of God."

"Allah is all-encompassing, all-knowing, all-seeing, Lord of the Worlds, Master of the Universe. Rahman is just one of the qualities that He possesses," Abi reminded me with a slight raise of his faint eyebrows, his look of gentle correction. He said the Qur'an had pinpointed ninety-nine such qualities, which are known as the ninety-nine names of Allah. "So when you hear Muslims talk or read from the Qur'an, you might hear one of these names in reference to the Creator," Abi said.

"So what does *rahman* actually mean?" I asked.

"Well, it has two interpretations," he said, putting a heel up on one of the stool's low supporting bars, pitching himself forward slightly. "Some people say 'compassionate' and some say 'beneficent.' They're really interchangeable, but I think 'compassionate' conveys the message of what Allah is all about more accurately," Abi said, and I made a quick mental plea to avoid the vocabulary lesson I feared my father was about to launch into.

He loved words and investigating their meanings and roots. He owned the biggest dictionary I had ever seen. It was easily ten pounds, as thick as two or three phone books put together, with tissue paper–thin pages and lettered tabs cut into the shape of half-moons along the edges. Its ivory canvas-like cover had bold gold lettering on the front, which, along with its heft and craftsmanship, gave the dictionary a sacred appearance at first. But as my siblings and I were made to fetch that anchor of verbosity and scour its many pages for the meanings of words we didn't know but should have, the dictionary's loftiness soon wore off. Luckily, Abi continued.

"Allah has compassion for all things," he said. "He cares for all beings. He's sympathetic toward the least of us, especially the least of us. You know what it means to have sympathy?"

He paused then, fixing his eyes on mine, waiting for an actual answer. I had to get the definition right or prepare to lug the dictionary upstairs.

"Yeah. That's like when you feel bad for someone who got sick or hurt," I answered. It was an easy word.

"Right," Abi said. "Well, imagine sympathizing not only with the sick or the hurt but also with the earthworms you all find in the lawn or a tiny ant crawling underground. Allah has sympathy for—or compassion for—all living creatures. He cares for and takes care of us all. That is why He is al-Rahman." There was a lightness to his voice, a shimmer of something like fulfillment that told me he enjoyed having this conversation, that he was glad I had asked. "You follow me?"

"Yeah," I said—and meant it.

Abi went on to explain that "al-Rahim" was another of Allah's names that meant, "the Merciful."

The rest of the prayer was an earnest plea: "Praise be to Allah, Lord of the Worlds, the Compassionate, the Merciful, Master of the Day of Judgment. It is Thee we worship, Thee we ask for help. Guide us along the straight path, the path of those whom Thou hast favored, not of those who earn Thine anger, nor of those who go astray." I wrote down the translation in the vocabulary clearest to me.

And I envisioned that path—freshly paved, lined with lush, well-manicured, verdant bushes, and unending—the next time I gathered with my sister, brothers, and father (my mother no longer joined) in the living room to recite our nightly prayer. While I sang the Arabic aloud, I listened to the English translation in my head. I felt then that the prayer meant more to me than to my siblings; I'd never seen Abi translate it for any of them. With my eyes closed, my hands cupped, and my family around me, I wondered if they could put as much feeling into the words as I now could.

8

Snapping

MY SISTER LOVED snapping on people. As a sixteen-year-old who could flit from hilarity to emotional breakdown nearly instantaneously, Aliya had a talent for delivering an insult with such novelty, humor, and insight that she could make bystanders, herself, and the subject of the diss all burst into uncontrollable laughter. One afternoon when I was eleven and we were in our room, she must have started snapping on me because I had a good comeback.

"Oh yeah? That's why you have no rhythm," I told her, then chuckled my way through an impression of her bouncing and bobbing awkwardly on our hardwood floor, pretending to just miss the imaginary beat I'd been trying to catch with a clap. I hardly exaggerated. My sister couldn't dance or clap on beat despite the stereotype that all black people can.

"Ha ha," she snickered at me, contorting her button nose, ample cheeks, and thinnish lips into a grimace. Sitting on her twin bed, neatly made with a reversible blue comforter, directly across the room from mine—identical, except not as neat—she nodded her head and flashed a furtive smirk that said she thought she had something better. "That's why you're an illegitimate child."

I laughed, at first, because her snap was funny.

How silly to be an illegitimate child of parents who'd had an elaborate wedding and lived as husband and wife for seventeen years, I thought. I kept laughing, longer than I wanted to, though, because it was also true.

Aliya had told me so when she found out, probably after eavesdropping on our mother on the phone—a favorite hobby of ours. Sometimes, when the phone rang and it was either Daily, Weekly, or Umti Khadija (who we didn't call "Monthly" because that's what my sister had named her menstrual cycle), Aliya would send me to hand Ummi the phone in her room, then we'd lurk in the hallway, close enough to hear Ummi's responses and sneak details about these women's latest dramas. Other times, when Ummi picked up from another line, Aliya or I would hold a hand over our receiver, then crane our heads together like lovebirds, lifting the phone until it touched both of our ears. We listened in like this for a few moments before our mother would catch on, whisper a "hold on, sis," and yell to us, "Hang up the phone!"

I was sure that it was during one of these listening sessions that Aliya heard my mother reveal that somehow—I didn't understand how—we were born out of wedlock.

Even though I trusted my sister, I needed to hear this news directly from the source. It was too important, meant too much, to accept secondhand. While I was riding in her car one day, I asked my mother to explain.

"I went down to the courthouse to file divorce papers against your father and the court told me I couldn't because your father and I were never legally married in the first place," she told me with slight exasperation at having to admit the truth to her child, a product of this "marriage."

"Well, why not?" I asked, confused.

"That answer is not so simple. You know that your father and I got married. Well, we had a wedding, an Islamic wedding. So we're married under Islam. But we never went to city hall to get a marriage license. I asked your father about it, but he always said, 'What do we need to do that for?'" she said in her deep, mocking-Abi voice, "and we never did it. After a while, I stopped asking. I figured that like most states, New York had common-law marriages, which is when a couple is living together like husband and wife for a period of time—a number of years—common-law marriage kicks in to recognize them as husband and wife even though they didn't go through the formal ceremony, you know?"

"Uh huh," I answered, trying to follow along with the technicalities.

"But the court told me that in New York State that practice is not allowed. Ain't that a blip? Imagine how embarrassed I was. Here, I want to divorce this man, and I can't even do it because we were never married in the first damn place. Excuse me, Feeya," Ummi said, pardoning her language. She reached over to place a hand on my arm. "You just make sure that you don't accept 'no' for an answer. If you know the right thing to do, don't let somebody tell you no, they're not going to do it. You keep on till they do the right thing."

With that, I knew that technically, my siblings and I were all illegitimate, just like Aliya had said, born to a mother out of wedlock. I felt about as far from being the loyal daughter of a once-loving couple as I possibly could. I used to search for confirmation that I was.

My mother cradles two clunky photo albums like a kitten in her arms as she plods into the living room, heavy on her heels, and sets them on the coffee table, one atop the other, for me.

"I don't know why you always want to look at these," Ummi says, already turning back to her room.

"Because, I like them," I answer as I raise myself on my knees, hovering above the square wooden tabletop while still kneeling on the floor. Picking the top album up with both hands, I place it in the table's mirrored center, out of the way. Its front cover was torn off long before it and I became acquainted, leaving only a curved, black, plastic *sheet lifter* guarding its pages from molestation. The pages are edged with gold and covered with crinkly clear cellophane that clings like static to adhesive black backing.

Both albums look old, older than I—at age six, eight, ten—and they are. Each is filled with small, squarish photographs with rounded edges of my grandparents, uncles, and my mother's cousins and family friends. Some of the faces I recognize, others I do not. No matter, those I don't know I ask about, and my mother has a story—she always has a story.

After a while, I hear them so many times that I learn to match the unfamiliar faces to familiar tales.

Whenever I open the other album, the one I really want to see, with the burgundy faux-marble cover bordered by two thin strips of gold,

I'm transported to the 1970s. There, near the front, is a black-and-white picture of my mother before she was my mother, when she was Joanna— or Jody, as relatives and old acquaintances sometimes call her. She's in profile, her chin held high, wearing a skin-tight shirt that reveals a pencil-thin neck on which she balances a huge Afro so thoroughly picked that pockets of air like thought bubbles take shelter in its coils. Looking at her—fierce, free, defiant—I see the resemblance, but my mother now is different.

My mother is sixteen in that shot, she tells me many times. She was dating a young radical named Nate. He had the most perfect Afro she had ever seen: round, neat, massive. Though I rather enjoy my reverie of him picking and patting it endlessly, I always roll my eyes upon his mention and that of her other teenage love, Pepé. My mother can't keep either name from slipping out her lips each time I open this album. She speaks about her memories with them as if they were the most fun she'd ever had, as if were it possible to go back in time with them to high school in the Bronx, she would—and leave my father and us without another thought. I quickly turn the page.

On another, my mother stands in a field wearing an ankle-length skirt, a crocheted poncho over a solid turtleneck, and a dark headscarf hiding any evidence of there ever having been an Afro. Her face—not smiling, not frowning, just looking—appears more youthful than in the Afro shot, but she is older, about seventeen, and becoming Muslim. There is melancholy in her posture, but I take something else from the photo: the promise of reinvention, of renewal, of commitment, for a higher purpose.

I flip the pages and more photographs follow: of my father skinny with a scraggly beard, his head covered with a kufi, and a baby I'm told is Aliya in his arms; and of Aliya, Isa, and me peering out the back of my father's Lincoln Town Car outside Nassau County Medical Center, waiting to bring our new baby brother, Muhammad, home. What I want to see, however, isn't on a page at all. Stuffed between the pages of this album are the contact sheets of my parents' wedding photos.

Time after time, I open the album to where the stack is tucked in and stop. I take the pile out, pick the pages up. There are three of them. Each is black-and-white with row after row of one-square-inch frames, proofs of some photographer's negatives from that day. They are the only pictures my parents ever show me of their wedding. They're the only pictures of their wedding my parents have ever had.

The most I can do to witness the start of my parents' marriage is peruse those proofs. At first, I can't make out many details of the ceremony at all. They're too small. Still I look, trying to detect, initially, some signs of affection between bride and groom, of happiness, of joy—something to prove and illustrate to myself that my parents had at one time, before I was born probably, loved one another.

Then later, when I know their union is ending, I scan for clues about what could have gone wrong with their nuptials, during their marriage, in their lives that would lead to them splitting up. I search for something, anything, amiss.

I lean in close to each matte-finished sheet and see nothing out of the ordinary. I see my mother, young and innocent, in a light sari and long khimar. I see my father, refined and trim, in dark Nehru-collared suit and embroidered kufi. I even recognize both sets of my grandparents, who don't often appear at the same time in the same place. Studying the succession of tiny squares, I notice long, rectangular tables covered in freshly pressed cloth and stocked with food galore; I witness a multitude of supporters, their skin black and various shades of gray, by my parents' sides. All seems to be in order.

Neither the wedding nor the reception suffered a mishap, glitch, or surprise that I can find. Instead, with the best wishes of their families, friends, and Muslim brothers and sisters, here is visual proof that my parents had indeed made a loving commitment to each other, in the name of Allah.

I close the album, for the moment, satisfied.

But recalling the photos left me confused. An illegitimate child had no father or didn't know who her father was. Mine had been known since birth. His name was on my birth certificate, although misspelled; "Abdur-Raham" it read. Just a mistake, I reasoned when I first saw it. But now I questioned whether the clerical error was accidental at all. What if Abi had given an erroneous spelling purposely, a false identity, so he could later deny my paternity? In fact, I allowed, maybe Abi hadn't ever wanted me—or any of us—around. Despite what I saw in the photos, maybe he never even loved my mother or us.

And although I was trying to resist blaming God, I felt confident that Islam—not only my father—was culpable for my illegitimacy. My parents' erroneous Muslim marriage would not have taken place without it. But it didn't make sense that the religion, by endorsing phony marriages, would willingly fail to protect my mother's rights as Abi's wife and mine and my siblings' as his children. How could Allah let that happen? Why would Allah, who controlled all things, make that happen?

Even though the lack of legal documentation of my parents' union may have had nothing to do with me, the reality of it called into question my entire being. Learning the truth, matter-of-factly, from my mother and hearing it starkly from my sister made me feel blurry, as if the borders that had defined me had suddenly become amorphous, barring the possibility of wholeness ever manifesting within or about me again.

Aliya and I got into one of our snapping sessions in our room on another day, and she repeated the joke that had quickly become one of her favorites.

"OK, you illegitimate child," she said, barely turning from folding clothes or choosing an outfit on her bed to face me in the middle of the room. It sounded mean-spirited this time, not like a snap. More like a put-down. Devoid of humor. It was the same joke, but not the same—decidedly different. Or was I?

I tried to be a good sport, to laugh, but my chuckles soon transformed into ugly sobs. My shoulders and chest heaved up and down. Tears and snot shot from my eyes and nose. I couldn't catch my breath. Moving closer to my sister, I plopped on the foot of her bed in an effort to compose myself but failed.

"Feeya, I was just kidding," Aliya said, trying to console me. "Stop crying. It was only a joke."

I practically convulsed with emotion. And when I couldn't stop, Aliya went downstairs to get our mother.

"What's the matter, Feeya?" Ummi asked, crouching before me.

"Leeya. Called me. Illegitimate," I sobbed with arms folded in front of my chest.

Releasing a chuckle, my mother tried to defuse the situation. "She didn't mean it."

"Yes, she did. I'm an illegitimate child."

"It doesn't mean anything," Aliya piped in. "I'm an illegitimate child too. We all are."

I didn't want to hear any more of her jokes.

"Feeya, just because your father and I weren't legally married when you were born doesn't mean you're an illegitimate child," Ummi told me.

"Yes, it does," I said with a giggle, inadvertently sputtering salty tears and snot into my parted lips, amused by the hollowness ringing in her consolation. "That's the definition of illegitimate. I looked it up."

"Well, your father and I were married in the eyes of Allah, and that's all that matters."

I looked at my sister in time to see her eyes roll. It dawned on me that her snap, although made at my expense, had been born from her own hurt. Aliya seemed to be saying that if she had to hurt, I would too. As sisters, we shared everything else: our room, her clothes, a language made from hums, our dreams, some secrets, and inside jokes. In the shame of our never-married, divorcing parents, we would also be bonded. And if she couldn't laugh about it, well at least neither could I.

"Right," I said. My mother had made a nice attempt. Her explanation managed to stay my tears temporarily. But it did not make me feel whole again. It would not erase the cynicism for Islam that our parents' marriage had instilled in my sister. And it could not explain to me Allah's culpability in my parents' fraudulent union. Considering how our lives were being upended because Ummi and Abi had only been married in Allah's eyes, my mother's justification was simply no longer—and, in fact, had never been—enough.

9

The Distance Between Us

RATHER THAN BEING separated in any of the ways I had imagined, my mother, my siblings, and I would all be leaving Abi. It was his decision to remain in the house where Aliya, Isa, Muhammad, and I had been growing up, alone.

Two of my uncles came over one day in early July, about a week after my twelfth birthday and sixth-grade graduation, to help us move. My father, as my mother must have suspected, did not interfere. We packed clothes, shoes, dishes, and books as fast as we could so my uncles could carry them out to the moving truck before Abi could do anything to stop us.

At one point, my oldest uncle, Wade, asked about the dining room table he kept having to maneuver around on his way to and from the truck: "Are we taking this table?"

"No, Hassan is keeping that," Ummi answered. Uncle Wade, wearing loafers, shorts, and an elastic-waist Polo shirt, continued to move other things.

Later, when the place was practically empty, the sky had darkened, and my second oldest uncle, Kenny, was sweating through his dingy T-shirt, he motioned to the dining room table. Nearly out of breath, he asked, "Should we take this?"

"No, that's Hassan's," Ummi repeated. Then she stared at the sturdy wooden slab patterned with coaster-sized squares over its surface. Rectangular strips of wood lay within each square; in one the strips faced horizontally and in the adjacent one, vertically, and so on across the tabletop like a wooden chessboard. This was where my mother had served Thanksgiving dinners, led my friends and me in drawing portraits and knotting T-shirts to tie-dye in a barrel on our back patio, and doled out many morning bowls of Cream of Wheat sweetened with brown sugar, butter, and milk. It was where my family regularly bowed our heads and parted our hands, uttering "Bismillah" and a short du'a before each and every meal. My mother thought for a moment, then seemed to be hit with a revelation.

"Yeah, why not?" she said. "Let's take it."

Uncle Kenny and Uncle Wade separated the table's halves with no effort and, in a hurry, each lugged his cumbersome piece out the front door. To stay out of their way, I stood aside on our hardwood floor and suddenly got a vision from before the floor was hardwood—when it was linoleum and my feet were planted in approximately the same spot they were then. The vision played in my head like a movie scene, dimly lit, frosty around the edges, gripping. I saw my parents—my mother on her back, my father standing over her. I heard the screams. I felt the fear. From the way it shook me, I knew the vision was a memory and nothing I'd made up, but where had it been? We hadn't had linoleum floors for maybe six years. How could my mind have buried this memory for so long? And why was it resurfacing now?

Everything seemed upside down or turned inside out. Our house, once filled with laughter, shouts, and prayers, was then emptied of five dressers, five mattresses and box springs, a sofa, a loveseat, the dining room table and chairs, all love, safety, and comfort. Looking around, I reflected on how Ummi told me people gained entry to Paradise after they died.

"There'll be a record of all the things you've done throughout your life, good, bad, and indifferent," she'd said, and I imagined an angel among the clouds of heaven holding a long scroll filled with this list. "And your good deeds will be weighed against your bad deeds." I saw an old-fashioned gilded scale, like the one the blindfolded lady of justice holds, only bigger. "If the good outweighs the bad, then you will be granted entry to Paradise. But if the bad outweighs the good, then . . . ," she shook her head. I remembered little Veruca Salt sliding down the bad egg chute in *Willy Wonka and the Chocolate Factory*.

Ummi told me I should do at least one good deed a day, not just because Allah was watching but because it was the right thing to do and I'd feel good about myself if I did. She'd remind me of this from time to time, particularly when I was being mean to Muhammad or in some way disrespectful to her.

"Have you done your good deed for the day?" she'd chime, in an accusatory tone.

My father, like everyone else, would face this Day of Judgment. And that fight I saw, regardless of the fact that I just remembered it, would appear on his record of deeds. So would this move. I wondered then where Abi's deed of driving us from our home would stack up on the scale of good and bad. Would it be counted as just a single bad deed or multiplied to reflect the magnitude of pain he was inflicting on my siblings, my mother, and me? Would he be able to do enough good in his lifetime to counteract the exponential dreadfulness of this one bad deed, turning us out of our house? Would he even care? I had no way of knowing, but I was sure Allah would not be pleased.

After we moved into our new house in Uniondale, about ten minutes away from where we used to live, my regard for Abi seemed to decrease every time he came to mind. Nearly whenever I closed my eyes, to sleep or even just to blink, I was assaulted with the memory of his imposing posture hovering above Ummi. I couldn't get over the fact that I hadn't remembered it. Without its coloring our interactions and my impressions of what he said and did, did I even know him—the real him— I wondered?

And I didn't care that our new house was almost just as good as our old one; I was still mad I'd had to move at all. I decided I could no longer talk to him. Twelve years old and powerless, the only means I could think of to get back at Abi for what he'd done was the silent treatment. It didn't matter that it seemed that I alone, among my siblings, was still upset with Abi for kicking us out. I alone harped on the injustice, unable to see a silver lining. So what. I would take my stand against him by myself. Days stretched into weeks and weeks into more than a month without my speaking a single word to Abi.

The summer I pretended I was not my father's daughter was nearing its end when Abi's mother, sick with emphysema from years of cigarette smoking, died. Only that forced me to finally give up my protest. I wore my sixth-grade graduation dress to her funeral. I had designed the knee-length white cotton frock that flaunted layered ruffles trimmed with a purple African print around my hips and thighs and a fat strip of it from the rounded neck all the way down the bodice. Sewn for me just two months earlier, it was already too small. I had grown so much since then, in development, maturity, and size. All day, as I sucked in my gut and carefully crossed my legs to keep the dress from riding up, my grandmother's friends approached me.

"Don't she look just like Louise?" they said.

I had heard it many times before while my grandmother was alive. We had the same medium-brown complexion, the same slender figure, similar dark hair and eyes, and our faces scrunched alike when we smiled. All this had earned me the nickname "Little Grandma." Normally, I was fine with it; in her sixties, Grandma bore a likeness to Ruby Dee at that age, petite, pretty, and powerful. She was something to admire. But that day, I shunned any comparisons.

Still, as I stood, milling about the church after the service ended, some stranger took my hand and led me, teary-eyed, to another stranger saying, "Ain't she Louise's spittin' image?"

I cringed. The last thing I wanted to hear while my grandmother lay motionless in a casket was how much I resembled her. But I went along with it all, smiling awkwardly.

Perhaps more uncomfortable than I was at the funeral was Abi. The denim and work boots I was accustomed to seeing him in had been replaced with a suit; he grinned, shook hands vigorously, reacquainted himself with old friends, neighbors, and relatives who called him Robbie instead of his name, Hassan, and hadn't seen him in years. I knew my father used to be Robert Nesbitt, just like my grandfather, and had changed his name when he became Muslim. I didn't know he had changed his personality too. His mother had just died, and he was friendlier and more pleasant than ever. He slapped backs. He gave hugs. *These people don't know Abi at all*, I thought.

The weirdest part was when he had to introduce us as his family. We all huddled close, hands and arms brushing against each other as though being posed for a family portrait.

"This is my oldest daughter, Aliya; my son, Isa; my youngest daughter, Sufiya; and the baby, Muhammad," Abi began, presenting the picture of familial perfection. "And this is my wife, Labiba."

My eyes momentarily bulged from their sockets. *Wife?* I thought. *Wife! After all we just went through, he has the nerve to still call Ummi his wife?* Was he so distraught by his mother's death that he couldn't remember booting his entire family from our home, including his "wife"? I was incredulous that he couldn't make his mouth form the little "ex" before "wife" and at least be somewhat accurate. Never mind that Ummi had never officially been his wife anyway. It was clear that Aliya, Isa, Muhammad, and I couldn't stop being his sons and daughters—and I even made a concerted effort to put my hurt feelings aside for the day to be there for Abi when he needed me—but this was too much.

Ummi, apparently unbothered, just stood there. She smiled and shook hands with whoever was getting the introduction, her two silver bangles, ever-present on her wrist, ringing joyously as she did. But she said nothing, did nothing, failed to make a single move to protect herself from what I saw as Abi's attack on her fledgling independence.

We left the church and entered the parking lot where our limo and Abi's new Pontiac Tojan sat ready to transport us to the cemetery to bury Grandma. Out of sympathy, I gripped Abi's hand. Once more, I allowed his head line, life line, fate line to connect with mine. But his fingers did not engulf mine the way they used to. They were still large with thick veins and flattened tips, but I was able to control their grasp. I knew I could let go at any time. As soon as Grandma was laid to rest, I told myself, I would release the feigned closeness of our folded fingers and resume the natural distance I now felt from my father.

PART II

10

Made Whole

MY FATHER WAS BORN Robert Nesbitt Jr. in Harlem in December 1950. The event effectively ended my grandfather's years at sea as a merchant marine, as my grandmother, Louise, attempted to make the three of them a stable home where little Robbie—as my father was called—could be raised up right. They lived in a corner apartment on the uppermost level of a six-story brick-and-cement building at the intersection of 115th Street and Lenox Avenue. My father had his own room. Across the hall, behind a set of French double doors, was my grandparents' room, and in a bedroom near the living room lived a family friend my father addressed as "aunt." His actual aunts, my grandmother's two sisters, were also close by, living in an apartment just down the hall. In Harlem, my father had all he needed and was quite comfortable.

While he did not, as people say, grow up in the church, he was raised a churchgoing boy. One Sunday morning, as was her habit, my grandmother turned the knob on her stereo and filled their apartment with the sounds of gospel tunes as she readied herself and my father for church. He heard the operatic tones of Clara Ward and the Ward Singers, their voices ringing with the sensibility of a Negro spiritual, as they affirmed "Surely God Is Able," and Sam Cooke with the Soul Stirrers wailing out a parable about a diseased woman's impassioned plea that Jesus could make her whole, if only she were permitted to "Touch the Hem of His Garment."

My grandmother wore only her best for church—that day, a dress that accentuated her slim figure, heels, and matching jewelry, offset with a coordinated hat that covered her dark curls and provided awning for the dainty features of her fallow face and dimpled smile. For my father, she chose a pair of stiff slacks, shined shoes, a crisp white collared shirt, and a tie she wrapped too tightly around his slender neck. He could not sully the clothes and this, for him, was reason enough to dread church.

Still, once dressed, my father and grandmother walked down the hall, bypassing his aunts' apartment this Sunday, and pushed for the elevator. The two always walked to service, just five blocks up Lenox Avenue to 120th Street. He saw other families out making similar strolls, all dressed in their Sunday best, the rhythmic clicking of their hard-soled shoes atop the pavement mixing with the rumble of the IRT line below. It seemed as though all Harlem was on its way to church.

They arrived at Mount Olivet Baptist Church, an almost square, pale stone slab with four huge, rippled columns out front, and went inside. My grandmother slid into a pew and crossed her legs. My father sidled up beside her and fidgeted, uncomfortable in the outfit that felt more like restraints than clothing. Recognizing that he'd become surrounded by adults who appeared completely absorbed in the churchly pomp and circumstance—in which he held no interest—he suddenly sought to flee.

"I want to leave," he whined, trying to steal my grandmother's attention from the pastor who had begun to speak. When all she did was shush him, he tried again. "Can we go now?"

But it was no use. My grandmother wouldn't budge. Just like everyone else lining the pews with transfixed eyes, she had become a statue who would do nothing but sit there. For an hour or an hour and a half, which to my father might as well have been forever, the choir sang, the preacher preached, and everybody just sat there. My grandmother forbade him from getting up or moving at all. When tears dribbled from his big round eyes, which were framed by faint eyelashes and sparse eyebrows, and rolled down his pudgy cheeks, it made no difference. He still had to be quiet and sit there. He would get no relief until the sermon ended and he could return to Lenox Avenue, finally free to move about.

As my father began to grow up, he recognized Mount Olivet less as torture and more as the place providing him a religious education. When he was old enough, he sat down in the church's basement, one point along the ellipse of Sunday school kids around the room, each grasping a thin booklet that depicted Bible stories in line drawings. On one page, Jesus ministered to the sick and needy. On another, his unmistakable long hair and loose robe hung as he delivered his Sermon on the Mount.

"If you accept Jesus Christ as your Lord and Savior," his Sunday school teacher said, "you will be saved." My father had heard him say the same thing the week before and the week before that. He'd heard it too from the pastor upstairs and the teacher in his Lutheran grade school. "Accept Christ as your Lord and Savior, and you shall see the kingdom of God."

It sounded so easy. Jesus was God. He performed miracles. He taught people to love thy neighbor. My father asked himself, *Who wouldn't accept Him as Lord and Savior?*

But at the same time, he realized that living according to the moral code to which Jesus adhered had its complications. After all, he was already barely dodging punishment for antics such as dismantling a pair of roller skates and using the wheels to make his own skateboard, lighting empty CO_2 cartridges to blast down the street like rockets, and once even melting the linoleum in his apartment when he started a fire playing with a metal lid and a canister of lighter fluid. He figured that was the real reason my grandparents sent him to church every Sunday: to learn how to be a good Christian, sure, but also to keep him out of trouble.

And he tried. My father was struck by the weekly morality lessons. The lives of Jesus, Adam and Eve, Abraham, Noah, and Moses, and their encounters with God, fascinated him and would continue to do so throughout his life.

But that was at Mount Olivet, my grandmother's church. My grandfather attended church elsewhere, and when my father went with him, he got a different sort of education.

My grandfather, Robert Nesbitt Sr., was born on March 5, 1918, in Macon, Georgia. He was one of eleven children, possibly more, but one of only eight who survived into adulthood. He and the seven of them grew up with his parents in a three-bedroom house in Jacksonville, Florida, with a single bathroom and no hot water. It was crowded but bearable until some of his sisters started bringing babies of their own into the already cramped space.

Bob, as my grandfather liked to be called, was one of the middle children. Headstrong and outspoken, he left school after eighth grade. A few years later, he grew weary of the constraints of living at home. He felt like a man and wanted to live like one. So one day, after working up his courage, he pocketed his oldest brother's seaman's card, made his way to a port along Jacksonville's St. Johns River, and walked up to a dock bearing the words NEW YORK in tall letters at its entrance. Posing as a seaman with the proper papers, the seventeen-year-old boarded a six-thousand-ton cruise ship called the *S.S. Iroquois*. At 410 feet long, it was the largest of the elegant Clyde-Mallory fleet, just right for my grandfather, the big dreamer. He tried to keep the fact that he didn't belong there a secret, essentially stowing away as the ship sailed—north to New York during summer and south to Miami and Havana during winter. But the crew soon took note of the new guy, who seemed just as lost on the massive steamship as a backwoods country boy on his first trip downtown.

"Do you know how to cook?" one merchant mariner eventually asked, not sure what else to do with him.

"Yeah, I can cook," my grandfather answered. Whether he actually could when he started sailing in 1935 is unclear, but he became a mess man, whipping up meals in pots larger than he'd ever seen for both passengers and crew. And everyone who knew my grandfather since then knew at least two things about him: one, he always spoke his mind, and two, in a kitchen he made magic.

With his middle school education, barrel chest, and wry smile, my grandfather soon joined the civilian seamen of the United States Merchant Marine. When a group of merchant mariners in 1937 formed the National Maritime Union, an integrated organization from the start, my grandfather—then nineteen—became a charter member. The union was the first in the country to guarantee equal hiring and pay for blacks. Black seamen also worked, ate, and slept alongside white seamen, unheard of at that time. In such a climate, my grandfather had the chance to earn promotions according to his skill and effort, instead of being barred from them because of his dark skin. He rose from cook to steward, and later, chief steward.

As World War II raged, he continued to sail, boarding ships involved in the American invasions of France, North Africa, and the island of New Guinea. Having previously never left the South, my grandfather wound up sailing the world seas for twelve straight years. Never would he return to live with his family in Jacksonville.

When he finally docked in New York City in 1946 at age twenty-eight, he was a well-traveled young man, keen to the ways of the world. As such, he was promoted to dispatcher at the Port of New York, then New York port patrolman, then agent for the Port of Baltimore, and later the National Maritime Union's national representative. The headstrong kid who had set out on his own, anxious to live a man's life, had earned just what he'd wanted.

My grandfather embodied the belief that it is hard work, not necessarily God or prayer, that yields rewards. Yet he attended Abyssinian Baptist Church, the gothic-looking worship house on Harlem's 136th Street and Seventh Avenue, regularly. The main reason: prestige. Abyssinian was arguably the most powerful black congregation in New York City. Adam Clayton Powell Jr., the congressman and activist, was its pastor. Services there were often just as much about politics as religion.

By that time in the mid to late 1950s, Rev. Powell was already known as an ardent advocate for racial equality and the advancement of Negro rights. He had represented New York in the House of Representatives since 1945, irritating many, both in the House and out, with his incessant activism and outspoken agitation for civil rights. In March 1952, for example, the National Council of Churches of Christ, to which Abyssinian belonged, voted to postpone a strong denunciation of the practice of racial segregation. When Rev. Powell found out, he was furious. He took to the pulpit and used all his ministerial menace to shame the organization.

"Christian ministers . . . have again crucified Jesus on the cross of bigotry and modern-day Judases have sold him for thirty pieces of white supremacy silver," he preached, his pale skin providing a stark contrast to his dark, shimmering hair that writhed and shook with his fervor. Rev. Powell got two thousand Abyssinian members to vote to withdraw the church from the council that Sunday. Although secession was not technically possible, Powell's point was clear. He demanded constant attacks on the country's practice of racial discrimination and expected his congregants, made up of civil rights workers and leaders, Northern advocates, and Southern transplants—such as my grandfather—to participate in the onslaught.

My father accompanied my grandfather to Abyssinian on many Sundays. For a while, church services were the only real time they spent together. And through them, my father became acquainted with the politicization of worship that he would, in fact, come to expect later in life. The few occasions he lost patience with it were when services let out and he thought he'd hop into my grandfather's car to get something to eat or just go home. Instead, he found himself stuck curbside, waiting for my grandfather to finish yet another discussion with the leaders of Harlem's various social and political organizations—my grandfather's friends.

Huddled outside the church stood men like Livingston Leroy Wingate, Congressman Powell's recruit to be associate chief counsel of the House Committee on Education and Labor; Percy Sutton, the famed civil rights lawyer who represented Malcolm X; and various heads of the Harlem chapters of civil rights groups to which my grandfather belonged, including the NAACP and CORE. Labor union rep Bob Nesbitt—my grandfather—was hardly the most prestigious among them, yet he was often the loudest in the after-church pack, cussing, cracking jokes, and arguing—but always with a smile—about how to overcome the latest societal ill that black people had been forced to endure.

All my father heard, however, was the familiar hum of his father's preoccupation with something other than him.

11

Breathe Again

ONE DAY DURING SECOND GRADE, my father came home from school to witness his life forever change. When he stepped off the elevator and approached his apartment, he saw the door already open. He saw men going in and carrying boxes and furniture out. He saw the home he recognized in turmoil, transformed into swaths of empty space, tufts of random dust, and stacks of cardboard cubes.

What is going on here? he wondered, standing in the corridor. *I left this morning and everything was fine.*

My father couldn't understand what could have happened in the short time he was gone that would lead to what he was seeing—which to him felt like nothing less than the capsizing of his entire life.

My grandmother, noticing him frozen in place, walked over to him.

"We're moving out," she said, in a tone that was not angry, but not comforting, and carried a tinge of condescension, which was her way. "It's going to be just me and you. Now come on before your father gets home."

She didn't explain why, didn't let on that she was furious. She just packed up all their belongings, and nearly all the furniture that my grandfather would surely miss, and moved herself and my father into a small apartment on Manhattan's east side that evening. Decades later, my father would be on the other side of such a hurried and hushed departure, but at that time, he was the kid being separated from his father, already beginning to yearn for his lost companionship.

My grandfather's presence, I would learn, was as significant to my father as is, for the rest of us, the existence of air. When it is there, all around us, sustaining and fulfilling us, as is its duty, we don't appreciate—or even notice—it, until suddenly, inexplicably, it's gone. And then we seize; our hearts arrest; we gag, gasp, and suffocate with grief at the intensity of our loss. We cannot breathe until some semblance of what was taken from us is restored.

My father's suffocation continued into the following year when, at around age seven or eight, my grandfather would show him the main reason for my grandmother's seemingly sudden decision to flee. During one father-son weekend, my grandfather took my father to an apartment around 155th Street, a bit further uptown from where they used to live, but near the black Lutheran school my father had once attended. Inside was a cute little boy with big round eyes, faint eyebrows, and medium-brown skin, all just like his own.

"Robert, this is Robin," my grandfather said of the two-year-old. "This is your brother."

Robin Nesbitt was born in 1956, the same year my father and his parents had moved back to New York from Maryland after my grandfather served two years as the National Maritime Union's agent for the Port of Baltimore. Robin's mother, Vivian, who had initially worked with my grandfather in the New York union office, had apparently stayed in Harlem while he was away. And Vivian was quite different from my grandmother, Louise. She wore her hair in tight brown curls, was thinner and fairer, and had a decidedly gentler, more reserved tone.

Eventually, after meeting them, my father was able to piece together that the reason he and my grandmother moved out, why he saw his father only on weekends, why his parents would never be married again, was because of that woman and her little boy.

Still, after spending his whole life alone, as an only child, all my father saw when he looked at Robin that first day was, at long last, a brother.

My grandfather, Vivian, and Robin would soon move into Hillview Towers, a condominium on 145th Street, the southernmost boundary of

Harlem's storied Sugar Hill, a neighborhood for affluent blacks. At their fairly new high-rise, a concierge was always present to greet them politely, and jazz songstress Dinah Washington was one of their neighbors. They had arrived at this "residence of distinction" because that year, 1959, my grandfather had become a National Maritime Union vice president— only the second black man to do so. A page-three article in *Jet* magazine with a picture of my bespectacled and mustached grandfather, wearing a self-confident smirk on his chubby face, announced his ascension.

Meanwhile, my father and grandmother moved into a two-bedroom apartment with an eat-in kitchen in the Bronx. They argued often, and to escape, my father—at nine years old—would begin taking the subway, a bus, or a cab from his home in the Bronx to my grandfather's Sugar Hill condo, by himself. He was certain that the solution to his problems with my grandmother pointed, like a compass needle, at my grandfather. Occasionally, throughout elementary and junior high school, when he felt stifled and fed up with the tension at home, my father would decide to run away. Always, he "ran" right to my grandfather's home. He hoped he'd be allowed to stay; there, he felt he might breathe again.

But to his dismay, my grandmother never let him.

12

Surrender at the Cinema

IT WAS THE MIDDLE of my school day—maybe third or fourth period—and I had just gotten settled in class when a messenger appeared in the doorway. She called my name, said I'd better get my things; I was wanted in the main office.

Haphazardly, I stuffed books into my bookbag while trying to match my guide's purposeful pace through the halls. I'd never been called out of class before. *What could the principal want with me?* I wondered, knowing I hadn't done anything wrong.

"Your father's here," the lady offered, reading my mind. "He said there's a family emergency."

I reached the office and Muhammad, who should have been at his school a mile away, was sitting there somberly next to Abi, who stood looking grave. He thanked the staff, and we three turned to leave without a word between us. In our silence, my heart beat with a strength I thought unnatural for a twelve-year-old girl but just right for a grown woman.

Though I wanted to ask Abi what had happened, I was too afraid to learn the answer. I'd already cried my way through the funerals of both of my grandmothers; I imagined soon having to bite my lip while standing at the casket of one of my grandfathers, too. Or, just as bad, we could have been on our way to visit Aliya or Isa, hooked up to ventilators and feeding tubes in a hospital.

We sulked toward my father's van. It was an ugly thing—rust brown with actual rust spots eating the metal overhanging the tires; a fat Mega

Blok—like body, not sleek or discreet in any way; tinted windows covered with blinds, as if anyone would want to peek inside after seeing the exterior; and on the van floor, a shag carpet in a medley of brown, orange, and white, completing the I-got-this-at-a-garage-sale effect.

It was a huge departure from the impeccable black Pontiac Tojan Abi used to pick us up in. All the kids lingering in front of the building after school would ooh and aah when it grumbled into the driveway. Like KITT from *Knight Rider*, it was low to the ground with a pointy front end, flat back end, and headlights that flipped up like blinking eyes. Ummi called the sports car "his midlife crisis." Abi got it when he was forty. By forty-one, he'd totaled it; and because—according to my mother—he hadn't bothered to get insurance, I was forced to ride around in that doo-doo brown, low-budget, *A-Team* knockoff van.

Still, I climbed inside. My face fell, becoming just as drawn as theirs in anticipation of the worst news, but then Muhammad and Abi burst out laughing. Broad smiles spread across their lips. My brother grabbed his sides. My father wheezed a little.

"Ha ha, got you," Muhammad said between guffaws, doubled over as if to emphasize the hilarity of their joke.

"I just needed a good excuse for taking you all out of school early," Abi explained.

"That's not funny," I said, trying but failing to repress a smile. "Then where are we going?"

"Ah, I can't tell you that," Abi said. "It's a surprise. But don't worry, it's a good one."

With the way I felt about him then, I couldn't have been less interested in my father's surprise. Every time he picked Muhammad and me up from school and brought us to our home, I was reminded that it was his fault we even needed a ride. We had moved twice since Abi booted us from his home: first to a house in Uniondale, where we started going to school, and now, a year later, to an apartment in Hempstead that was too small, had mice, and wasn't even in the district where my mother still sent Muhammad and me to school. I would have preferred not to go anywhere with Abi that day—or any day. But he was my father; I didn't have a choice.

I stared out the window, searching for clues to reveal where we were going as we drove out of one Long Island town and into another. Part of me was a detective, trying to discover our destination without being told; the other part, a protector keeping track of our route in case Muhammad and I needed to make a run for it. Whatever we were doing, why couldn't it wait until after school, I wondered? I continued to study the streets and note landmarks along our way, dropping breadcrumbs.

Deeper into Hempstead, I knew of only a handful of places we visited nearby—the flea market, Western Beef, the African American Museum that never seemed to be open, a black bookstore, White Castle, and the movie theater. Everything we passed so far was familiar; I thought if Abi was trying to escape with us, he wasn't doing a very good job of obscuring his route. When we made a right onto North Franklin Street, I became pretty sure we were just going to the movies.

The Hempstead theater was small, run-down, and practically unknown to people who didn't live nearby. It was almost always nearly empty, but just beyond a corridor of wood and metal scaffolding along the sidewalk that led to the ticket window, I could make out a small line. I'd never seen one there before. When we got to the front, Abi spoke like a king commanding subjects with his resounding depth: "One adult and two children for *Malcolm X*."

So that was why we were there. It was opening day for Spike Lee's biopic on the influential Black Muslim leader that everyone on the news and in the streets had spent all summer and fall of 1992 talking about.

I had seen the baseball caps emblazoned with the letter X that vendors along Harlem's 125th Street were selling. I'd admired the huge posters picturing Malcolm X in browline glasses with his pursed lips, dimpled chin, and pointed finger above his famous words, BY ANY MEANS NECESSARY. I'd noticed men wearing T-shirts portraying him in various poses with an array of profound quotes. The movie seemed to have resurrected the man so well that there was almost a movement surrounding *Malcolm X*; I didn't think anybody in the black community—let alone my father—would miss it. Going to the movies was probably his favorite pastime, and Malcolm, his hero.

We had to be first.

"What you'll see in this film is more important that any lessons you would have learned in school today," Abi said, leading us inside.

We sat down a few rows from the screen in seats lumpy, dingy, and gray. The material was so worn I couldn't tell for sure whether it had once been velvet, but I suspected it was. Duct tape covered tears in several places, but at least the colors matched. I wriggled around until I found a spot where springs weren't poking me too hard in my butt and back, then questioned whether we were there to support a theater in a black neighborhood or because it was the only one around that would show *Malcolm X*.

At first, staring up at the screen watching Lee and Denzel Washington sway down a street in zoot suits was not quite what I expected from a movie about the transformative minister the country had largely tried to erase from memory, but it was entertaining. The whole theater crackled with laughter when Detroit Red jumped out of his chair, feeling the sting of lye as he got his hair conked. We laughed harder when none of the faucets worked, and Red eventually had to dunk his head in toilet water to relieve the burning.

Just before the intermission, I sat rapt watching a militant cadre of brothers from the Nation of Islam soundlessly stand guard amid a screaming mob. The protestors rallied outside the hospital where a black man lay after being badly beaten by police. Officers were on edge, thinking they'd soon have to quell a riot. But when Minister Malcolm dispersed the unruly crowd with a simple flick of his leather-gloved hand, my father beamed. He leaned over, his black leather jacket crunching under the weight of his movements, and told me, "That's just how it was," as if he'd actually been there.

By the time Malcolm X found Sunni Islam, I was lost in the film. His transformation from street criminal to dogged purveyor of black pride to man ensconced in self-discovery through his recognition of the humanity within Islam was confusing and yet made total sense. This man was tortured by his past, his rough upbringing, and by his everyday existence as a black man in a country that didn't respect black men. He needed Islam. It saved him.

In submission, Malcolm knelt inside a beautiful chandeliered and red-carpeted mosque during his pilgrimage to Mecca. He prayed in Arabic. From my lumpy seat, I mumbled the words along with him.

"*Bismillah al-rahman al-rahim,*" we opened the prayer.

Except at mealtimes, I hadn't prayed with anyone since moving out of Abi's house. I wanted to, but the shape of my family had bent, folded, and severed under the pressure of Abi's absence. My sister, Aliya, who was entering her senior year when we moved, largely ignored me as she spent all her time out with friends or on the phone with them. My older brother, Isa, who didn't want to change schools and mess up his straight-A record or abandon his horde of friends, eventually, out of convenience, just moved back into Abi's house. By the time I'd entered eighth grade that year, Aliya had gone off to college, and only Muhammad, my mother, and I were left living together. My family had split up, just as I'd feared.

I longed to forge my faith connection again. But Abi had always been the one to facilitate our prayers, gathering us in the living room to sit on sheet-covered couch cushions in our pajamas before bed each night.

"*Alhamdulillahi rabbi-il al-amin. Al-rahman al-rahim.*"

At the new house, I had sometimes lain at night—with the lights off and my sister's often empty bed across the darkened room from mine—whispering the prayer to myself or reciting it soundlessly in my head before I fell asleep.

"*Maliki yawmi din. Iyyaka na-buduwa, iyyaka nasta'iyn.*"

But I had begun to forget some of the words. I always stumbled at the same point, losing the melody and my train of thought after I reached: "It is Thee we worship, Thee we ask for help."

I tried forcing myself to remember, to recall the mingling of Abi's baritone with Ummi's harmonic alto in my head as I used to hear in our living room. But it was hard to conjure what was no longer there. And I doubted that my little brother, across the hall from me, remembered how to pray. Nor did Ummi, who always fell asleep hours before me anyway and sometimes used to let Abi's calls to prayer go unanswered, seem like the right person to ask to join me. Without my family surrounding me and with my unfettered connection to God then broken, I felt alone in my Islam.

So even if only listening to a celluloid character recite the prayer, it felt good to hear someone else utter those words again. In them, I sensed Malcolm X's complete surrender to the will of Allah. It was just a movie, but the scene made me reach back through time and space, to traverse fantasy into reality, and truly feel for Brother Malcolm and, through him, reconnect with my faith in God.

"*Ikhdinas siraa-til mustaqim,*" he continued.

That was it—guide us on the straight path. I read the English translation of the prayer in white type along the bottom of the screen, checking it for accuracy while taking note of the Arabic phrasings that had escaped me. As I did, I wondered whether the rest of the theater felt as profoundly for Malcolm X as I then did.

In time, I mouthed with him, "*Walla-dau leen. Amin,*" closing the prayer.

Listening to that meditative recitation of the prayer, labored yet uplifting, gave me back something I hadn't realized I'd lost. It filled me with warmth, though I hadn't noticed I'd been shivering. It struck me then that maybe by taking Muhammad and me to see how Malcolm Little became Malcolm X, and Malcolm X became El-Hajj Malik El-Shabazz, Abi was trying to show us how and why he became who he was. Why, at times, he struggled to control his anger. Why he demanded so much from us and from blacks as a whole. Maybe why he'd been attracted to Islam—and to Ummi, his Betty—in the first place.

I realized that perhaps Abi didn't want us only to watch the movie but maybe to see in it some of ourselves as well, some of our heritage. In *Malcolm X*, the movie, and more importantly, the man, I had discovered a link to who I was as a Muslim.

This was worth leaving school for. I don't know whether he meant to, but Abi managed to begin replacing the image of him that had haunted me for months. And in the process, he'd finally given me a reason to stop being mad at him: He revealed that he cared enough about me to teach me about myself.

Leaving the theater, Abi, Muhammad, and I maneuvered around a small crowd of people that had amassed outside, waiting for their chance to watch Malcolm Little transform into El-Hajj Malik El-Shabazz. Among them, I felt as if I'd been part of something special.

"How was it, brother?" one older man with a graying beard asked Abi as we passed him in line. A black-and-gold patterned knit cap encircled his head. He might have been Muslim. Looking at Abi with his own beard and a baseball cap shielding his head, the man might have recognized that we were too.

"Great," Abi said, guiding Muhammad and me into the street with a light touch of his fingers on our backs. "Powerful."

13

The All American

BY THE END OF SUMMER 1965, both my father and America had started down a path of change from which neither could detour. That March, the country went into shock when it watched Alabama state troopers and members of the Dallas County Sheriff's Department trample and beat the mostly black peaceful protestors marching across Selma's Edmund Pettus Bridge for the right to vote. That August, residents of the predominantly black neighborhood of South Los Angeles called Watts, stunned the country when they revolted against their constant degradation at the hands of police, among other injustices, in a violent six-day rebellion that would live in infamy. The turmoil would leave thirty-four people dead and injure more than one thousand.

At the same time, though, blacks rejoiced at winning the right to vote. Congress had passed the Voting Rights Act, opening up possibilities for African American voices to finally ring in the political and justice systems, deaf to such concerns for too long.

Meanwhile, my father had just spent the summer living with my grandfather, my uncle, and Vivian at the house they'd recently bought in Teaneck, New Jersey. Just a short drive from New York City, Teaneck was a safe, quiet, suburban enclave for those Harlem blacks who had "made it." Jazz musicians Nat Adderley, Stanley Turrentine, and Yusef Lateef all lived within blocks of my grandfather's new home. New York Giants offensive tackle, Roosevelt Brown, whom my grandfather affectionately called Rosey, lived next door. The R&B singer Chuck Jackson had settled there, as did the popular Isley Brothers, who named their label, T-Neck Records, after the town.

As summer waned and the prospect of starting high school back in the Bronx loomed, my father couldn't fathom leaving Teaneck behind. He thought my grandmother should let him live with his father and go to high school there. To him it made perfect sense, considering that he never wanted to live away from my grandfather in the first place. He approached my grandmother.

"I don't want to go to that school," he told her.

"Well, that's where you're supposed to go, Robbie," she said.

"It's not even in walking distance," he complained. "Why can't I go out to Jersey and stay with my father?"

"What do you mean, stay with your father?"

"Well, I could live with him in Teaneck and go to school out there," he answered. "They have a house with enough room for me. The high school is huge, and it's on a beautiful campus. And it's the suburbs. I stayed in the city for junior high. Isn't that enough?"

My father, fourteen years old and transitioning from boy to young man, steeled himself for an outright rejection or at least an argument, but one didn't come. My grandmother simply listened.

Then, sounding weary and resigned, she said what he'd been waiting seemingly forever to hear, "All right, Robbie."

He figured he'd made a good case. He thought she saw the logic in his well-reasoned points. My father didn't consider, however, that maybe his mother was tired of fighting with him. That maybe she was worn out with trying to convince him to stay with her when it was obvious that all he wanted to do was be with his father. That maybe she recognized that her only child, her little boy, was nearly a man but could use the guidance of his father to fully become one. And so, she let him go.

After the unexpected cleaving, followed by years of separation, my father returned to his father and finally felt free to breathe.

Coming from a South Bronx tenement building where he could smell his neighbors cooking arroz con pollo and hear the treble of salsa music alongside their arguments—whether he wanted to or not—my father quickly absorbed the comforts of upscale Teaneck. The kids there experienced an upbringing different from the one he was used to. In the beginning, when the promise of possibilities abounded, he felt that, at last, he was living the life he'd always wanted.

He went to parties, rode his bike, did his best James Brown impression, and wrote and recorded songs beneath the basement staircase of my grandfather's home with the new friends he made. They were so close, it was as if my father had gone from being an only child to instantly having more than a half-dozen brothers. He decided they would make themselves into a club called the All Americans, like the 82nd Airborne Division of the US Army, a patriotic band of brothers.

On weekends, my father led his All Americans into the neighborhood to wash windows, rake leaves, mow lawns, and hose down cars for a fee, trying to earn money so they could buy patches with the double-A logo he'd designed and matching burgundy, double-breasted blazers they would all wear as their club uniform. The boys cherished their unity, their exclusivity. Together, they felt they were an unstoppable force of cool.

But as he matured through high school, my father's priorities shifted. His fledgling upper-middle-class lifestyle, incongruent with how he was raised in Harlem and the Bronx, would cause him to question just who he was as a young black man. Sights he'd overlooked for months and years he now saw with new eyes. All around Teaneck and nearby Englewood, for example, attractive homes with verdant yards were guarded by waist-high lawn jockeys. The statues of small black men, forever outfitted in a service role, kept interminably on their feet and maintaining a self-sacrificial outstretched arm, were offensive, my father suddenly noticed. When he was sixteen and seventeen years old in 1967 and '68, they were an image of himself he no longer wished to see daily.

So in his senior year, after he got his driver's license, my father decided to take a stand. He, his cousin Greg, and several other friends from the All Americans piled into his 1959 black Mercedes for a nighttime drive around the nearby white neighborhoods. Each boy kept his eyes trained for houses with black lawn jockeys out front.

"There goes one," Ernie, Rodney, or another All American might have announced upon spotting a statue.

"Stop the car. Pull over, pull over," Greg added in a stage whisper.

My father cut the headlights and crept the car over to a curb a few houses away. They didn't want to get too close in case someone was watching. Then, giddily, Cubie, Java, or another All American dashed out, sneaked up, and smeared white paint all over the too-black, lantern-grasping lawn jockey's subservient little face. With wetness dripping from its chin, the small man stared back at the grown boys, ghostly and grotesque. As they slipped away, my father reveled in the dumbfounded gaze he imagined would appear on the homeowners' faces when they awoke to find their beloved black Jockos turned white.

14

The Awakening
(Mood Blue)

⟨

AT SEVENTEEN and just months away from his high school graduation, my father began dabbling in the civil rights plight that had for years engulfed blacks nationally, despite his own relative immunity. Really, there would be no more escaping it.

When he traveled from Teaneck to Harlem to visit family or catch a Jackie Wilson or James Brown show at the Apollo, he always encountered suit-and-tie-wearing street-corner preachers from the Nation of Islam. His natural curiosity caused him to stop and listen—for at least a few moments—as they touted the Honorable Elijah Muhammad's teachings, his "message to the Blackman," his debasement of whites. At first, the rhetoric went in one ear and out the other, but gradually my father began to ponder what he heard. Were blacks truly God's chosen people? Was the Nation of Islam really the cure to the spiritual, psychological, political, and economic ills that plagued the black community? At the time, the role of religion in my father's life was becoming like a rearview-mirror image—it shrank smaller and smaller as he continued to move forward until he'd gained such a distance, he could no longer even make it out. On Sunday mornings, for example, when many of the All Americans took a break from each other to attend church, my father sat at home.

For years, he'd been shepherded to Baptist, Methodist, Pentecostal, and Catholic services with his mother, his father, aunts, and cousins—

and even served a yearlong stint as an Episcopal altar boy at his and his mother's church in the Bronx. But now, he had fallen out of the church-going practice. His friends who went to church each Sunday didn't seem particularly concerned with remembering or serving the Lord on other days of the week. Not that they were heathens. They did things that normal teenage boys did: went to dances, worked on their cars, rehearsed singing routines, spent the occasional night with a girl. There just never appeared to be a thought of God in any of it.

My father remembered the omnipresence of God that all those hours in church and Sunday school had taught him. Yet it seemed that people's knowledge of the Almighty had little bearing on how they actually behaved. He began to question whether there was a point to the Christian practices he had been brought up in, or whether the Christian teachings he'd learned were even true. *Was Jesus really born on December 25?* he asked himself. *Is Jesus God? Was he the son of God? Did he die on the cross? Did he give his life for people's sins?* Not even the central canon of accepting Christ as Lord and Savior to gain the kingdom of heaven made sense to him anymore, if it meant that someone who'd never heard of Jesus could, for that reason, be doomed to hell.

If he couldn't fully believe in Christianity, was there any truth to this Nation of Islam religion, he wondered?

Based on the prominent green-domed mosque at 116th Street and Seventh Avenue, the bustling Nation of Islam businesses, and the clean-and-pressed Fruit of Islam he saw all around Harlem, my father figured there might be some. So he handed over his twenty cents to buy a copy of *Muhammad Speaks*, the Nation of Islam's newspaper, and a quarter to pick up *The Black Panther*, the paper of the Black Panther Party for Self-Defense, whenever he was in the city. Through them, he learned of the need for jobs in the black community, fair pay, access to housing, and lunch programs for school children. He was particularly drawn to the full-page illustrated centerfolds in *Muhammad Speaks*. They depicted the schools, hospitals, markets, and other infrastructure the Nation of Islam wanted to build to make its own communities, independent of whites and white dollars. Those drawings allowed my father to imagine what might be possible if black people banded together to create opportunities of their own. And looking at the programs the Black Panthers developed and how they carried themselves, he got even more of an idea.

This is what I'm talking about, my father said to himself when he saw the Panthers—many of them teenagers like him—on TV, marching around sporting black leather jackets and gripping shotguns in the crooks of their arms. *Tell these people you're not gonna have it.*

But as he sat alone on his basement couch watching TV after school on April 4, 1968, he was jolted from his delusions about the civil rights struggle and his place in it. A news bulletin broke in. A reporter announced that Rev. Martin Luther King Jr. had been shot and killed. My father couldn't take his eyes from the screen.

The sky outside darkened, turning the room blue in mood and color. The television glowed with coverage that evolved from the special report of King's death to retrospectives about his life to accounts of riots breaking out around the country in response, and my father could only watch. He watched as his shock became sadness and sadness became grief. He watched as the nation's grief transformed into anger and anger into rage.

Sitting there, immersed in the tragedy, my father was forced to honestly take stock of his own involvement—or lack of it—in the fight for equal rights. All around him were symbols of his absence from any kind of struggle: the console TV set before him that his father could afford with the salary from his prestigious job; the couch he sat on, where previously he and his friends had gathered as the patriotic "All Americans"; the house in Teaneck itself, awash in privilege and adequately distanced from communities labeled "underprivileged."

Suddenly, it struck my father that he wasn't a player in the battle for equality at all, only a spectator. He had no say, held no sway. As powerless as he had been as a little boy, forced by his mother to endure incomprehensible and seemingly interminable church sermons, he was again as a teen watching the news of King's assassination—able to do nothing but be quiet and sit there as tears rolled down his cheeks.

It was late by the time my grandfather came home. My father was still distraught from the news and couldn't imagine how my grandfather felt.

For perhaps the first time, as my grandfather approached, the civil rights background noise that my father had ignored his entire life was finally full blast; he recognized that he had no choice but to pay attention.

"We lost a good man today," my grandfather said, uncharacteristically reticent.

"Yeah," my father responded, saddened and embarrassed.

15

Black Revolutionary

(

MY FATHER HAD ARRIVED on the campus of Bethune-Cookman College in Daytona Beach, Florida, in late summer 1968 looking like the seventeen-year-old kid he was: about five foot six but still growing, with heavy eyelids over slightly protruding eyeballs, a thick lower lip, clean face, and half an inch of neat, tightly coiled hair ringing his head, with a part through the left side. Yet, despite his youth, the freshman marched into the local market he'd heard complaints about, armed with pad and pen. He took note of dust-covered boxes and rusty canned goods lining the shelves. He approached the white man ringing customers up at the counter.

"Why are you selling these things to the people in the community?" he asked, as if he were Perry Mason interrogating a witness.

"What?" The man looked puzzled. "Are you here to buy something?"

"No, I want to know why you're selling these inferior products to the people."

"If you're not here to buy something, then you had better go. Before I call the police."

That stunt earned my father a phone call from my grandfather: "Boy, what are you doing down there?"

My father thought he was trying to help. He had resolved, when he graduated high school, that he'd go off to college and find ways to participate in solving the race problem; he promised himself he'd do whatever possible to get involved in the ongoing black revolution. So he asked around campus about Bethune's Afro-American Student Union and started attending its meetings and events. He made friends with some members, and he and his cousin Greg, who enrolled at Bethune-Cookman at the same time and roomed with my father freshman year, even began demonstrating with the group; once was when Daytona Beach planned to desegregate its public schools through busing. My father and Greg joined angry Volusia County parents protesting a court-ordered 1969–70 school-year initiative that bused mainly black students to wealthy, predominately white schools on the waterside section of town; they were arrested. Daytona Beach police officers handcuffed them and took them to the jail in town.

"Name?" the booking officer asked my father.

"Robert X. Nesbitt," he answered. He thought that using the Nation of Islam moniker, "X," was a clever first step toward identifying himself with the struggle against white oppression. From their posts behind bars, my father and the other young radicals felt more legitimate—and quite secure; they puffed their chests and periodically taunted their jailers: "You pigs!"

The cops made no response.

By morning, my father, Greg, and their cohorts were released and returned safely to campus. Yet soon my father's attachment to both the campus and his cousin began to slip. Seeing less and less purpose in attending classes and otherwise participating in college life, he moved out of the dorms and into a cottage off campus. There my father contemplated his next moves. Enamored with the possibility of self-sustaining black communities promoted by the Nation of Islam, he started removing the designs for hospitals, schools, and businesses from the centers of *Muhammad Speaks* and taping them to the wall behind his new apartment's bed. One picture went up neatly beside another. And then above. And then below. Week after week he did this until no more wall could be seen, only plans.

On either side of those plans, he hung two floor-to-ceiling banners that a girlfriend had made from huge strips of red, black, and green nylon fabric, the colors of the African liberation flag. Red represented the blood African people had shed fighting for their freedom; black was for their skin; and green, their land. Together, the colors were meant to symbolize the unity of African peoples everywhere. As my father lay down each night and awoke each morning, with the source of his dedication hovering in bold imagery about his head, he would not forget the commitment he had made to uplifting his people.

Emboldened, my father made more forays into battling injustice. One such opportunity came when he and his Afro-American Student Union compatriot, Bobby, pulled into a Daytona Beach gas station one night. They were sitting in the new turquoise 1969 Mercury Cougar XR-7 that my grandfather had recently bought him, waiting to fill up for quite a while, when Bobby mentioned that he saw other cars pulling in and getting serviced right away.

"Did you see that?" Bobby asked.

"What?" my father said.

"That gas station attendant. He went over to that other car. They pulled in after us and he's serving them."

"Oh, don't worry about it," my father said, trying to calm his friend, who was clearly losing patience, but then it happened again. Bobby stepped out of the car.

"How come you wanna serve them?" Bobby shouted at the attendant.

"I'm gonna call the police," the white attendant said.

By then, my father had gotten out of the car too. Although his days of burgundy double-breasted blazers were gone, the two were dressed similarly, in young renegade attire. My father favored a khaki safari jacket to which he affixed a button featuring either a teeth-bearing black panther, Malcolm X, or the outline of the African continent. Wrapped around his wrist was a black liberation wristband he'd made from a black leather strap partially covered with red and green electrical tape. He'd grown his hair into as much of an Afro as his perpetually stunted strands would allow. And over it, he occasionally wore a black beret like a Panther. He wasn't a member but considered himself an affiliate.

"Yeah, that's good. Call the police. I'd like to talk to the police too," he told the attendant.

A few minutes later, a squad car pulled up with sirens blaring. A white officer who stood about six foot two got out, approached the gas station attendant, and began listening to the man tell his story, arms flailing in animation.

Let me go over there and tell him my side of the story before he gets just one side, my father thought as he approached the officer. He began to speak: "Excuse me, officer, but—"

The cop whipped around, pointed a long finger in my father's face, and said, "Boy, if this man doesn't want to serve you, he doesn't have to."

Insulted, my father could not contain his composure: "Motherfucker, fuck you!"

The cop moved swiftly, yanking my father's slim five-foot-seven frame up by the back of his shirt and belt buckle, slapping handcuffs around his wrists, and throwing both him and Bobby into the back of the squad car as they continued to scream and cry foul.

It could have been worse. My father had forgotten where he was. He'd forgotten that not even ten years earlier, when he'd traveled South to visit Greg and his brother Rodney in rural Florida, he hadn't been allowed to sit in the same movie theater seats as white patrons. He'd forgotten being scared silent after a white man driving a pickup truck in this Florida town named by Native Americans, whom whites had nearly silenced long before, had reprimanded him for calling out to a white girl on the street. He'd forgotten that a little more than ten years earlier, a black northern teenager had been brutally beaten, shot, and his body mutilated, weighted down, and thrown into a Mississippi river after being accused of whistling at a white woman. He and Bobby only had to spend the night in a Florida jail. The next day, a public defender represented the two young activists and they were let go. My grandfather didn't even find out.

16

Malcolm X Resurrects

THE DIM ROOM BRIGHTENED with black-and-white images of a man with a strong jaw, piercing stare, and accusatory fingers. As the speakers broadcast his message condemning injustice, inequality, and the lesser station blacks occupied in America, my father—seated among his Afro-American Student Union peers—lost himself in the deliverer's voice. Rich and resonant, its tone could embody the comfort of a father when it needed to and the indictment of a prosecutor if so inclined. It was full of passion and commitment, shaped by knowledge and experience.

Malcolm X may have been dead for more than four years by then, but he was born again to my father in 1969, when he first watched documentaries about him during gatherings at Bethune-Cookman College. In his pitch, his phrasings, and in Malcolm X's unyielding diction, my father found a leader who would guide him on his journey to upset the status quo. As someone new to activism, he heard in Malcolm X's voice an exemplar worthy of fervent study and admiration.

Over the following weeks and months, he began to learn about Malcolm X, the man. My father's childhood home, he discovered, was just a block from the Lenox Avenue street corner where Malcolm X used to stand atop a soapbox preaching to passersby. *Muhammad Speaks*, the newspaper that first exposed my father to proposals of black independence and whose illustrations wallpapered his bedroom, had been Malcolm X's brainchild. Malcolm X even had six children, the same number my father imagined he would have himself one day. To my father, it felt as though fate eventually led him—or led him back—to a man with whom he felt such kinship. Especially when he reflected on the reason for the rest of the country's fascination with the stately young minister: all that he had the nerve to say.

"Revolutions are never fought by turning the other cheek," he once said, and in the next breath dismissed civil rights tactics used by activists based in the black church, tactics steeped in harmony and pining for integration. It was as if Malcolm X were speaking my father's mind.

"Revolutions are based upon bloodshed. Revolutions are never compromising," he added, noting the potential lethality of these endeavors. In such words and in the rasp in Malcolm X's throat by the end of an impassioned speech, my father recognized a quality unlike anything he had ever heard before.

"Revolutions overturn systems. And there is no system on this earth which has proven itself more corrupt, more criminal, than this system" —the American government—he charged. Malcolm X had the audacity not to couch his discontent in Bible verses or old Negro spirituals, not in undeserved forgiveness or unchecked conciliation. No, he stood with it, was awash in it, allowed it to steel his spine and furrow his brow. His conviction about this sense of profound dissatisfaction and his refusal to rest until he gained satisfaction on behalf of black people forced my father and everyone else to take notice. There wasn't an inch of pretense in Malcolm X's commitment, and that drew my father in.

Soon, he would devour all the information he could find about Malcolm X. If there was some film, he'd watch it. If there was some audio, he'd play it. If there was an article, he'd read it. Years afterward even, when there was a movie, he, of course, rushed out to see it. He was locked into Malcolm X and his message.

Malcolm's philosophy of Black Nationalism especially resonated with my father. It started with the "so-called Negro" people engendering enough pride in their African ancestry to finally accept who and what they are. Only then, according to Malcolm, could they become intellectually independent enough to think and feel for themselves, first individually, then collectively. As a united force, people of African descent would forge their own freedom "by any means necessary," gaining complete control of the politics, economics, and the social and cultural emphasis of their own community, Malcolm X said. This Black Nationalism, of black people doing for themselves, was what my father saw pictured in photographs lining the pages of *The Black Panther* and what he envisioned rising up from the illustrated centerfolds of *Muhammad Speaks*.

Now that the dream of Black Nationalism had nestled within him, filling the crevices between his heart and mind, it was what my father noticed was missing from his experience at Bethune-Cookman and the purview of its student body—despite its being a historically black college. His role as student activist, he realized, no longer gratified him. *Why am I here? What am I doing?* he asked himself, depressed by his tendency to impotently highlight the plight of black folks when he'd enrolled determined to discover a solution.

He decided it best to leave school and further investigate the Nation of Islam, where ideas for remedies were abundant. If he was in the Nation, at least he could make those blueprints of businesses and schools on his bedroom wall real. Even if nothing was built, he knew that becoming a Muslim would change the entire structure of his life, from his inner values to his outer demeanor.

So one day, my father packed up some clothes from his cottage apartment, loaded several bags into his Cougar, pawned his conga drum and a few other trinkets he kept in case he needed fast cash, and drove himself an hour and a half north to Jacksonville, where he had once seen a Muhammad's Temple. It was the closest Nation of Islam mosque he could think of.

He only briefed Greg about what he was up to: "Don't tell anybody," he said and left.

He rolled into town after dark. All the businesses were shuttered and not many cars were on the road. My father drove along until he saw an open door and a group of young people inside with Afros, wearing clothes like his own. He thought they were holding some sort of a rally. He parked the Cougar and went in. The people inside were indeed holding a Black Power rally, and my father fit right in. He struck up a conversation with one young man.

"Hey man, I'm Robbie. I just got into town and I been kind of looking for something like this," he said. "I don't have a place to stay yet."

"I'm staying with this preacher," the young man offered. "You could probably stay here with us." And for the next several nights, my father—fledgling Black Muslim radical from Harlem, New York—bunked in the home of a white Catholic priest in Jacksonville, Florida.

Meanwhile, after being unable to reach my father, my grandfather in Teaneck began calling around—to Greg, the school, and to my father's friends—trying to find him. But nobody would tell my grandfather where he'd gone.

"Y'all gonna tell me! Somebody gon' tell me something," he wound up yelling into the telephone instead.

Back in Jacksonville, my father felt fortunate to have met the young man who'd invited him to stay at the priest's home. He didn't know where he would've gone otherwise. And the two got along. But after he chatted the young man's ear off about what the Nation of Islam does to empower black people and how Islam seems to be more all-encompassing than Christianity, the young brother had a warning for my father: "If you do plan on joining the Nation of Islam, you know you're not gonna be able to keep wearing that cross."

He was talking about the gold and diamond crucifix that dangled from a gold chain my father wore around his neck. It had been a confirmation gift from his mother. She handed it to him following a ceremony at St. Paul's Episcopal Church in the Bronx when he was twelve. Since then, my father had worn the cross every day. It reminded him of the relationship his mother had wanted him to forge with Jesus, that of a friend. He couldn't imagine turning his back on Jesus, which is how he thought about taking off the cross. Yet he had to face facts.

Looking down, he realized, "You're probably right."

Still, when he felt comfortable, my father ventured out to the Nation of Islam temple he'd driven all the way from Daytona Beach to find. It was a Sunday, and the temple was abuzz with activity, harkening back to his churchgoing days. But the extent of the similarities stopped there. Unlike at church, a security guard positioned at the temple entrance searched him, along with everyone else coming in, patting him down for weapons and perhaps wires. Once satisfied that he was clean, the guard directed him inside.

Dozens of folding chairs neatly arranged in rows greeted him in the worship hall. Women wearing ankle-length skirts and head coverings that flowed to the middle of their backs sat on one side. Men, mostly in dark suits, white shirts, and slender ties, sat on the other. My father joined the men, instantly impressed by how organized and orderly the service appeared. The minister soon took his place at the podium and delivered his sermon. Long on praise of the strengths of black people and denigration of the injustices committed by whites, the Nation of Islam message lived up to its promise. Satisfied that he was getting what he came for, my father decided he would return to the temple the following Wednesday.

On that second night, a security guard searched him at the entrance just like before, but this time, without even viewing any identification, the man asked, "Are you Robert Nesbitt?"

Hesitating, my father faltered a response, "Yeah," he said, his voice quavering. "How do you know who I am?"

"Your father was here looking for you."

My father's brief puzzlement was followed by a sudden and intense dread. If his father had come all the way down to Jacksonville, Florida, from Teaneck, New Jersey, he knew his adventures as a college dropout and Nation of Islam hopeful were coming to an abrupt end. He went into the service anyway and sure enough, in the midst of the preaching, my grandfather showed up.

My grandfather wasn't a very tall man. He was rather stout and round, with a midsection that ballooned like the hula hoop on clown pants, but he was nothing to laugh at. His lips could curl from beneath his mustache and his eyes could burn from behind his glasses. His real power, though, was in his sharp tongue and booming voice. When he decided to raise the volume, his words were like thunder—clapping ferociously and striking fear into entire neighborhoods. And his language could be just as fearsome, filled with profanity and an impropriety he got away with because who would dare challenge him? (It was these qualities that made me particularly shy around my grandfather; I was nothing like him and wanted to avoid calling attention to the fact.)

My grandfather waited until the service was over and brought my father back to his hotel to tear into him. It started with just a look, or rather *the* look—the one of a parent's major disappointment that could make any child crumble into self-loathing. And then the lecture began: "Boy, what are you *doing*?"

My father wasn't supposed to answer that. He sat with his head bowed, prepared to take the tongue-lashing that came in a barrage of unanswerable questions: "What the hell is wrong with you? What the hell is on your mind? How the hell could you go and . . ." And then my grandfather, who'd only had the chance to finish eighth grade, got to the bottom line. "Boy," he said, "don't you know I put out all kinds of money for you to go to school? And here you are."

My father could only sit there while my grandfather made it clear that no son of his was going to quit college to become some black revolutionary.

By the end of his tirade, though, my grandfather began to marvel that he'd even been able to find my father after driving all around Jacksonville with Greg, looking for a turquoise Cougar, until they spotted it parked outside the Nation of Islam temple. My grandfather noticed the irony in my father's hanging around what used to be his own stomping grounds back when he lived in Jacksonville years earlier. My grandfather's anger gave way and he chuckled.

"Boy, I used to rip and run these streets myself."

Despite the coincidence, his father would not allow him to squander the education he was so generously trying to provide. My grandfather insisted that my father return to Bethune.

Reluctantly, my father complied and completed his sophomore year. But his heart wasn't in it. While he was supposed to be buckling down academically, instead he studied Islam.

He didn't buy into what he'd heard while visiting the Jacksonville temple. The ideals of discipline, self-respect, self-defense, and Black

Nationalism were solid. He'd read about and agreed with as much in Elijah Muhammad's books, *Message to the Blackman in America* and *How to Eat to Live*. But the Nation's theology gave him pause. My father had a hard time squaring that Elijah Muhammad, a sharecropper from rural Georgia, was the Messenger of Allah or that a door-to-door salesman turned preacher named W. Fard Muhammad was Allah, the Creator himself. On top of that, the Nation of Islam was in some way responsible for his hero Malcolm X's death. Three members had been tried and convicted of the killing a few years earlier. After learning who Malcolm X really was, no longer thinking of him only as the firebrand he heard about on the news, his assassination left my father heartbroken, although four years had passed since the rest of black America's heart broke for Malcolm. He just couldn't get comfortable with the idea of joining the Nation of Islam.

The process of self-transformation through adherence to certain principles that the Nation of Islam promoted, however, intrigued him. Those principles—prayer, belief in one God, abstaining from alcohol and fornication—my father learned, came from the Islam of the Prophet Muhammad, Sunni Islam.

By studying, he started to see that the Prophet Muhammad's Islam was so much larger than Elijah Muhammad's Nation of Islam. Suspecting that it might hold the solutions to the black man's plight that he'd been seeking, my father decided that when he finished school that year, he'd go home and figure out the true Islam.

17

Becoming Muslim

BACK HOME following his second and final year at Bethune, my father had a good idea of where to start his search for true Islam. The last time he was home in New York, he bought some books from the Nation of Islam's Harlem bookstore. Their inside covers had been stamped with the location of an Islamic center—72nd Street and Riverside Drive.

One day soon after he returned, he drove his Cougar down to the Islamic Center, walked into the five-story Upper West Side townhouse, and greeted the Middle Eastern men there who welcomed him. Within a few moments of speaking to them, my father made it clear that despite being American and black, he'd done his research and was knowledgeable about Islam. One of the men, the sheikh, then interrupted their back and forth: "Do you want to take shahada?"

My father knew this to be the official means by which one converts to Islam.

"Yeah," he answered without hesitation.

First, the men took him to a washroom and showed him how to make wudu, the ritual cleansing that Muslims perform before praying. Then my father repeated the statement that all men and women must declare in order to embrace Islam: "Ashadu an laa illaha illa Allah. Wa ashadu anna Muhammadan rasul Allah." I bear witness that there is no god but Allah. And I bear witness that Muhammad is the messenger of Allah.

With that, his search was over. It seemed so simple.

Well, now I'm a Muslim, my father told himself as he left the building.

He felt proud, slightly concerned about his ability to quit pork without another taste, but ready to start experiencing an Islamic life. His first act would be to locate people like himself, black American Muslims.

He remembered earlier when he'd tried to visit a mosque in Harlem. Although it was closed at the time, on the door he saw a circular red, black, and green sticker—like the flag he'd hung on his Daytona Beach bedroom wall and the wristband he was wearing when he was arrested at a Daytona Beach gas station—that stuck in his head. He thought about it again as someplace the new Muslim him should know.

So he got back in his Cougar and drove uptown to the International Muslim Society at 303 West 125th Street. This time, the mosque was open.

Inside, an older black man was teaching two young black women something in Arabic. The young ladies appeared very studious. My father was instantly impressed; the two of them were the first black American Sunni Muslims he'd ever encountered. He approached the teacher and expressed his interest in Islam.

The man then asked him, "Do you want to take shahada?"

"Well, yeah," my father answered with only slight hesitation. Again, he repeated the statement to declare his embrace of Islam: "Ashadu an laa illaha illa Allah. Wa ashadu anna Muhammadan rasul Allah." And for the second time that day, he became Muslim.

This time, the sheikh decided to give my father, who at the moment was still Robert Nesbitt Jr., a Muslim name. My father had listened to, watched, and read Malcolm X's statements about shedding the white man's names many times before. "We believe the black man should be freed, in name as well as in fact," he'd said. The Nation of Islam preached that blacks should free themselves of the surnames of their former slave masters and used an "X" to represent the unknown African name that had been stripped away. This was because, as Malcolm told blacks of the 1960s with all the urgency one would use to alert another his house is on fire, "Murphy is not your name. Jackson is not your name. Smith is not your name. Bunche is not your name. Powell is not your name. That's the white man's name." On his own, Malcolm went even further, advocating for names that reflected African and Muslim heritage, "names that don't

connect you with the white man but names that connect you with God."
He'd said, "Those names give you honor."

Somehow, the sheikh settled on Hasan for my father's first name, which means one of handsome character, and Abdur-Rahman for the last, servant of the Most Compassionate. The Arabic name was a mouthful, but my father indeed felt honored to have been chosen to exemplify God's compassion.

Accepted then by tiny cohorts of both Middle Eastern and black American Muslims, Hasan Abdur-Rahman, my father, felt like a real Muslim, doubly official. At last, he was confident he had settled on the right path. There was nothing holding him back now from progressing in his effort to uplift the black community and himself.

That was 1970, nine years before I was born. My father was nineteen years old.

PART III

18

The ABCs

ISLAM, I HAD DECIDED, was mine. It was my birthright and my destiny. The possibilities for who I was and who I could be—newly in possession of a kernel of understanding of where I had come from—seemed boundless. Because no one else in my family wanted to lay claim to this identity at that time, I decided that I would. Having reclaimed my heritage and forgiven my father's wrongs, I swelled with the potential for wholeness I now possessed. I approached my father with this newfound resolve.

"Abi, can you teach me Arabic?" I asked him when I got to his house after school one day. I was in ninth grade at the high school that Aliya and Isa had attended back in Baldwin. In classes, I sat beside, before, and behind some of the same kids I knew from elementary school. I still lived in an apartment in Hempstead with my mother and younger brother, but the high school there was so bad it had been listed as one of New York state's failing schools. My parents would not allow me to go there. And since our schools in Uniondale had already kicked my brother and me out for no longer living in the district, my mother decided to drive us about fifteen minutes back to school in Baldwin in the mornings and pick us up from Abi's house, where we used to live, in the afternoons.

"Why do you want to learn?" Abi asked me with a slight chuckle.

I figured that learning Arabic—the language of the Qur'an and of Islamic scholars worldwide—was necessary to gaining any real knowledge of the religion. Deciphering the language of Islam could be key to piecing together and fully envisioning the jigsaw jumble of the faith before me. But I didn't want to tell Abi, Mr. Ten-Pound Dictionary, that. He might expect too much of me, like fluency within a matter of months. So I hedged.

"Well, I want to learn enough to at least write my name in Arabic," I said, "and maybe, one day, I could read the Qur'an as it was originally written. You know, not translated."

Abi was then on what was becoming an increasingly common furlough from his job as a union electrician in construction deficient, early 1990s New York City. Sitting at home in his undershirt, essentially out of work, he often didn't have much to do. Perhaps considering this, along with the likelihood that his book-smart daughter would make a worthy student, he got on board.

"I don't remember much," he said. "But I'll teach you what I know."

Immediately, we sat down at his dining room table. Patterned with coaster-sized squares that alternated between horizontal and vertical strips, like a wooden chessboard, it was identical to the table in our own apartment, the one Ummi took as her due when we moved out of Abi's a couple of years earlier. Apparently Abi hadn't been ready to part with it and had bought himself a twin. He ripped a piece of paper from a small spiral notebook, laid it on the table, and sketched each character of the Arabic alphabet, along with the sounds they make in English, in a couple of lengthwise columns. He cleared his throat with the familiar clap and rumble of thunder that so easily signified his presence. Then, with a straight face and a serious manly tenor, he sang a little alphabet ditty.

"*Alif, ba, ta, tha, jim, ha, kha . . .*"

I listened as intently as I could but quickly felt a giggle bubbling up. I tried to contain it, but it was irrepressible.

"What's so funny?"

"Nothing," I said, still chuckling. "It's just weird hearing you sing the alphabet. It's, like, for babies."

"This is how we learned it at MIB," Abi explained. He was in the habit of mentioning MIB from time to time. He spoke of it with fondness and a distinct exaltation, albeit a persistent lack of specificity. But by then I knew it was the mosque where he and Ummi had converted to Islam. What the imposing capital letters "MIB" actually stood for, though, escaped me. "We had a really good Arabic teacher there, the best. All the brothers learned from him."

I imagined a room full of bearded black men wearing kufis and long tunics, squeezing themselves into wooden desks designed for children, not for the broad shoulders and long legs of grown men. Yet I recognized that Abi's bringing up MIB, an organization he clearly respected, was my cue to get serious again.

"Now repeat after me," he said. *"Alif, ba, ta . . ."*

But I cracked up, open-mouthed and doubled over, nearly falling out of my chair. It was too funny. Abi sang each character as if he were at auditions for Juilliard: so earnest, so determined to find the perfect pitch. He couldn't let go of his penchant for gravity even in singing the alphabet. I had to let him in on the joke.

With much concentration, I sat up, held my breath, and focused on the letters of the alphabet long enough to stop laughing. Then, staring at Abi, I lowered my tone and imitated his basso profundo rendition in mock solemnity. When Abi smiled, perhaps realizing how stern he sounded, I switched to a note that harmonized with his. We were like a Middle Eastern Motown as we scaled through each character again and again.

Eventually that day, I learned the Arabic alphabet. But my recitation did not exude nearly as much candor or passion as my father's.

19

Facing Destiny

(

MY FATHER WAS IN a taleem class at the mosque at 303 West 125th Street, where new Muslims got educated on the fundamentals of Islam, such as salat and the Qur'an. He'd just closed the composition book in which his instructor, Hasan Abdul-Hamid, had written in Arabic the section of the prayer he was practicing that day, along with its Arabic transliteration, and was preparing to collect his shoes from the front doorway.

Then a group of young black men walked in. There was one russet-skinned brother of average height with a full beard, wearing a patterned kufi and long buba stepping out in front, and a small entourage of similarly garbed men who flanked him on either side. They strode into the mosque like a band of soldiers: straight-backed, stern-faced, briskly paced, and all their footsteps nearly synchronized with one another.

Oh boy, these brothers here, my father said to himself, impressed with the group's entrance. *Who are these guys?* And he approached the apparent leader of the pack to find out.

"As-salaamu'alaikum," he said.

"Wa'alaikum as-salaam." The brother identified himself as Imam K. Ahmad Tawfiq of the Mosque of Islamic Brotherhood.

They were the ones my father had been hearing about. It was their circular black, red, and green logo with a sword, a star and crescent, and Arabic script in the middle affixed to the door that had initially drawn him to the building he was then inside. That symbol was a combination of black and Muslim pride, the very things my father was reshaping his life around. He thought that whoever came up with it were people he needed to know.

"I'm new to Islam," my father told Imam Tawfiq. "I just took shahada here recently."

"Yeah? Alhamdulillah."

"Right. Well, I don't know any other blacks in Islam, but I'd like to find some. Where can I go to find others like you?"

"Come down to the jummah here, brother. We'll be back. And lots more like us, masha' Allah," Tawfiq said before turning and leaving, his small entourage in tow.

Given everything my father had experienced on his way to becoming a Muslim and all the purpose he was still searching for as one, he knew he wouldn't miss that Friday's jummah.

There's so many of them, my father thought as he entered the mosque. Until then, his exposure to black Muslims was limited to the handful in his taleem class and one man who'd visited his mother's house to help with a correspondence course he was taking. Yet inside the Friday service there were dozens of them, at least a hundred. There were some Middle East-erners and a few who looked Hispanic mixed in, but just about all the other Muslims there were black like him. My father was amazed.

After removing his shoes and performing wudu, he walked over to where the men were gathered and crouched with them on the floor to listen to the khutbah.

The imam he'd met the other day, who'd invited him there, stood at the front of the room. Once everyone had settled in and directed their attention toward him, the imam opened his mouth to speak. Every word was Arabic.

My father could hardly believe it. A black American man whom he found out was just in his early thirties could speak perfect Arabic? Instantly intrigued by the worldly knowledge this man possessed, my father sat rapt.

Upon finishing his Arabic sermon, Tawfiq translated his message into English in a subdued tenor tone with a subtle Southern accent. He spoke of struggles in the black community—with justice, with jobs, with safety—and related them to stories of the Prophet Muhammad's life. He addressed relationship issues and emphasized Muslims' adherence to the hadith. In a familiar black vernacular, he touched on topics that everyone could relate to and made Islam accessible to all the newcomers looking for someplace to belong.

My father was inspired. In this Mosque of Islamic Brotherhood, or MIB, he had found what he'd been looking for. As the service ended and he replayed its highlights in his head, he left the mosque knowing for sure that he would return.

20

My Father Said So

MY FATHER LIKED RUNNING for exercise and maybe for a chance to get away from everything and everybody but us. He took my siblings and me with him on these runs, usually two at a time—either Aliya and Isa, who had both run track in high school, or Muhammad and me, or sometimes just one of us alone. But Aliya was too far away, living in the Bronx then; Isa was off at college in Washington, DC; and Muhammad had never taken an interest in track. So this morning—and we always went early mornings—Abi was taking only me. He called me as he left his house in Baldwin.

"I'll be there in ten minutes," he said. "Meet me in front of the building."

"All right," I said, even though I didn't want to run. I could not refuse him.

My mother, my little brother, and I had recently moved from Hempstead to a new apartment in Freeport. It was only slightly closer to Baldwin Senior High School, where I now illegally attended eleventh grade by continuing to use my father's address. But we at least each had our own bedroom, although still the occasional mouse.

Hanging up the phone, I opened my dresser and found a pair of wind pants, the hand-me-down sports bra I'd gotten from Aliya—my only one—and a T-shirt to throw on. I slipped on my silver hoops, the only earrings I had that fastened and didn't tug my earlobes when I ran, and hustled out to the living room. My mother approached as I sat on the couch to tie my sneakers: "Aren't you going to eat something?"

"No time. Abi said he'll be here in a few minutes."

"He can wait while you eat. You shouldn't run on an empty stomach."

"No, Ummi. I gotta go."

She ducked into the kitchen anyway, and I heard her opening up drawers, the fridge, the oven. Just as I got to the front door to leave, she emerged with a foil-wrapped biscuit from the batch she'd baked the day before. "Here, take this with you," she said, stuffing it into my hand. "You can eat it in the car."

"All right, Ummi. Thanks," I muttered. I was sixteen and exasperated by but grateful for Ummi's incessant mothering.

I took the elevator downstairs and climbed into Abi's already waiting van. About fifteen minutes had passed from the time he'd called, though he said nothing about my lateness. We exchanged good mornings but not much else. It was too early to talk. Too early to be outside. Too early to even be awake on a weekend. But there we were.

Abi turned his van onto the curvy highway entrance ramp, and I held out hope that we were going anywhere but The Lake. I wasn't up for that long run or all it entailed on this morning. Within minutes, though, we reached the nearly three-hundred-and-sixty-degree roundabout exit into Hempstead State Lake Park, "The Lake." Slivers of the water's surface glistened through abundant foliage tinted a deep purple and seemingly ready to drop. From the passenger's seat, I took in the view because I knew that once we started jogging, all I'd see was tree bark and dirt. I had made this run before.

We pulled into the parking lot, nearly empty save for the hardest of hardcore runners and one or two equestrians taking their horses out for an early morning trot. I bid farewell to my hopes of a laid-back weekend as we left the van and looked for a clean spot to stretch.

I did all my favorites from track practice—a calf stretch, leaning with bent arms into a tree trunk; a quad stretch, holding each knee up to my chest—partly to prepare my muscles for the run and partly to show Abi that after a couple of years on the team, I knew something about running. Then we hustled onto the path. There were two of them: an asphalt jogging trail and, on the other side of a narrow strip of trees, a dirt bridle path. Both encircled the large pool of water for which we dubbed the entire park "The Lake." Abi chose to bypass the trail especially made for runners and instead made it part of our experience to dodge horse crap, twisted tree roots jutting from the ground, and the occasional mounted beast along the dirt path.

"I don't know why they make these jogging trails out of concrete," Abi said. "It's terrible on your feet, your legs, and your back. Every time your foot hits the pavement, it sends shock waves through your whole body. The dirt is a natural shock absorber. It offers just enough resistance and support for your strides."

"Uh-huh," I said, winded. I didn't understand how Abi, at forty-five years old, could manage to say so much while running when I could barely get a word out, trying to breathe and keep up my pace at the same time.

"What do you guys run on for practice?" he asked.

"Both," I answered, then paused. "When we run through the neighborhood," I said in one big exhale, "we run on the sidewalk." After another pause and big inhale, I continued, "Sometimes," pause, "we run on the grass around school."

"Can you tell the difference?"

"Yeah," I said, although I had never thought about it before. I just didn't want to hear Abi's response if I said, "No."

"Good. Then you should tell your coach to let you jog on the dirt all the time. It's better for you. Tell him your father said so."

We ran on for a while, and I tried to find my rhythm, looking for a balance between pumping my arms and taking long strides while breathing deeply and not bouncing too much. Meanwhile, Abi had reached the part of his jog when he turned around and ran backward. Backpedaling, his legs cut through the air like scissors, heels first, toes sweeping the ground, and still managing to propel himself ahead of me. The positioning was meant to work different muscles in his legs, Abi explained. Though admirable and a feat of discipline and self-control, the backward running still looked more to me like showing off.

"And you see, you're running on your toes. No wonder your shins hurt. You're running like a sprinter," Abi said.

"I am a sprinter."

"To run distances, you have to get off of your toes. Plant your whole foot down when you take a stride. It'll distribute the pressure."

I tried letting my heel hit the dirt as I ran. It did feel a little bit better, but my body still hurt, especially my heart, which felt as if it were beating twenty times too fast and would jump out of my chest at any moment.

"Come on, keep up," Abi said when he saw me beginning to lag behind. "We're almost there."

Abi's chats during our jogs were as much a part of the training as the actual running. They were usually broken into three sections: first, the mechanics of running; then, the conversation shifted to matters of spirituality; and finally, he wrapped up with his thoughts on the pertinent social or political issue of the day. It seemed as if we'd been on the trail for hours by the time Abi got to the spiritual part.

"I don't understand how people can look around and not be amazed by all that Allah created," he said breathlessly as we plodded along the dirt, side by side now. At last, he was becoming winded. "The trees, this dirt, the air. The Creator created all of this." But Abi waved his arms around and still had enough energy to conjure a smile. He continued, "And there's beauty in all of it. And there's a purpose for all of it." Abi gave the example of perhaps a tree, whose roots absorb water from the soil, which allows it to grow leaves that provide shade as well as food for insects and birds. When those leaves take in sunlight, they're able to produce oxygen for us to breathe and also to help clean the air. It's a perfect symbiosis between living things. He noted there were other examples of Allah's perfection throughout nature. "You just have to look around you. It's all around you."

Listening to the rhythmic thump of our footsteps against the ground, I wondered why Abi was telling me this. Did he think I didn't know or hadn't considered it before? Or was he telling me about the wonders of Allah because he thought that I, more than Aliya and Isa before me, could appreciate what he was saying? Abi wasn't saying anything I didn't also believe and occasionally marvel at myself.

To prove it, I gave my own example.

"Well, you know the planet, is mostly water, with all the oceans and lakes and rivers and stuff?"

"Yeah," he said, as we blew past a slower jogger.

"It needs all that water for the land and the plants, and so people and animals can drink and wash themselves," I said, repeating something I'd heard in science class.

"Right, exactly. This is what I'm talking about," Abi cut in excitedly. But I wasn't done yet. Over the years, I had spent hours listening to Abi—on these runs that ate up weekend mornings and during phone conversations that often killed handset batteries. He was always doing the talking and I, the listening. But this time, I was ready for him to hear me out. I stopped him.

"Wait, Abi, I wasn't finished. The human body is also mostly water."

"OK," Abi said, giving me time to get my words out now.

"It needs all that water to live. You see, what we need, we can get from what God gives us. That harmony is Allah's design."

Abi shot me a look with raised eyebrows and wrinkles furrowing the skin beneath his receding hairline. I had momentarily shut him up.

Smiling, he said, "I didn't know you thought about those things."

Mildly insulted, I said, "Yeah, Abi. All the years you've been talking, I do actually pay attention sometimes."

"Well, good. Then you've completed Hassan's School of Spirituality. We can stop going on these runs. I'm getting too old for this anyway."

Had I known that all I had to do to end the running torture was speak up for myself, I'd have done it sooner.

But that day, we ran on—with me ready to collapse from exhaustion at any moment and Abi fading, though only enough to be noticeable. After I spent too many minutes looking ahead for the end of the trail, Abi entered the third and final segment of his talk, the political portion.

"America is not going to let a black man walk free if a white woman has been killed and the black man is suspected of killing her. It doesn't matter if he did it." Abi spoke as though the subject had given him an extra jolt of energy. He was upbeat enough to even make jokes. "The man could be innocent, but if he's the one that white people say did it, then he did it. Guilty. Case closed. Send him to the chair," Abi said, and we both laughed. "And O. J. Simpson had the nerve to be married to this white woman? Forget about it. There's no way he's getting off."

Watching nonstop coverage of the 1995 Simpson trial on cable news would soon become Abi's favorite pastime during his latest furlough from his electrical union job. He'd have all sorts of theories on the case and argue them as if he were one of Simpson's attorneys himself. The drama of the trial thrilled him, like everyone else in the country who watched, but I think its racial justice implications and how Abi had witnessed their evolution within his own lifetime gripped him even more. Perhaps that's why on another run we discussed the controversy surrounding *The Bell Curve* and on another, Ebonics, and on another, how America had accepted a rapper into its living rooms weekly but only when tamed by the forces of wealth and flanked by a family who appeared to reject the typical cultural markers of blackness on *The Fresh Prince of Bel-Air*.

By then in that day's run, though, Abi had total control of the discussion. Too whipped to even attempt forming a complete sentence, I had simply given up on talking. The truth was I hated running distances. Aliya, Isa, and I were all primarily sprinters, and running anything longer than a mile, for me, was a form of torture akin to a level of Hell. So later, when I found out the true distance of the path around the lake, I was not surprised that Abi never revealed it was four miles long.

He must've known that with that knowledge, he couldn't have forced me into his van for those jogs, let alone gotten me to accompany him willingly. My main reason for going in the first place was to spend time with him. With track practice after school and friends on the team I sometimes visited afterward, I wasn't at his house long before Ummi came to pick me up and bring me home each day. The least I could do was not argue when he called for a jog. Still, whenever I was on the path, I always strove to finish it or at least run farther than I had the last time.

Panting, sweating, and trudging along in the dirt, at last, I spotted a break in the trees and could make out patches of pavement up ahead. We were nearing the parking lot—the finish line—so I pushed forward, propelled by the burst of adrenaline I usually felt at the end of any race.

Noticing my resurgence, Abi said, "Let's go around again."

"No. Abi. Please. I can't," I begged, my legs turning to anvils crippling me instantaneously. I doubled over with my hands on my knees, my chest aflame from a heart overworked. But Abi just kept moving.

"Come on, you can do another lap," he said running backward to face me as he launched back into section one of the run talk. "Breathe. In through your nose. Hmph. And out through your mouth. Whew." He was several paces ahead of me then, jogging farther and farther away from the van. Watching my father's frame shrink as it approached the expanse of Allah's creation and was soon engulfed by the grove of parted trees bowing slightly to welcome his presence, all I could do was take a deep breath and drag myself after him.

21

Long-Distance Mentality

MY FATHER STOOD IN his old bedroom in his mother's Bronx house staring at the gleaming gold pendant with a diamond in its center that he'd worn every day on his chest since his confirmation at twelve years old. He didn't want to put it on anymore. Since taking shahada and joining the Mosque of Islamic Brotherhood, he felt that he couldn't. Like the young man he met at the Jacksonville rally had warned, my father realized now that the pendant, a cross, symbolized Christianity, Jesus. How could he come from listening to Imam Tawfiq's khutbah about the Prophet Muhammad and Islam's relationship to the black community, he wondered as he eyed the ornament, and still display this Christian relic of the white Jesus being crucified for man's sins?

His mother gave him that cross, though. She was so proud of him then. And he didn't want to disrespect her or make her feel he didn't appreciate her gift by taking it off. Still, the cross just didn't represent who he was anymore. My father considered simply not wearing it, sticking it in a drawer and never looking at it again. But in accepting Islam, he wasn't rejecting Christ or Christianity. One reason he had become Muslim was because Muslims recognize Christianity as a predecessor to Islam and Christ as a prophet of Allah. He wouldn't denounce the religion. He just had to figure out what to do with the cross.

One day, as his involvement with the Mosque of Islamic Brotherhood grew and his faith as a Muslim solidified, my father took the gold pendant and gold chain, walked over to his mother with it hanging from his hand, and, without saying a word, placed it in hers. It hurt. He felt the loss immediately, and the growth, like a cicada shedding its shell, which had both bound and protected it, and unfurling its wings, delicate and fine, for the first time. Giving her back the cross, he knew, was the best possible solution.

And his mother accepted the gift without any fuss. From that day on, he saw her wear three pendants—her cross, a Star of David, and his cross—all close to her heart.

With his connection to the church securely behind him, my father was ready to delve into Islam without reservation. One such way was to join the rest of the brothers for their Saturday morning exercises. Imam Tawfiq had created a fitness regimen to help instill in mosque members self-respect. After all, Tawfiq taught that as black people they were not the second-class citizens that many had perceived them to be just a couple of years out of the civil rights movement; instead, he called them Kushites, members of the powerful African Kingdom of Kush that had once ruled ancient Egypt, spawning both male and female black pharaohs. They were the oldest race on earth, the mother of civilization, Tawfiq said. They, the Kushites, were something to be proud of.

My father arrived outside Tawfiq's squat Brooklyn apartment building that first day with this in mind. He strode over to the dozen or so brothers, many in their early twenties or late teens, as he was, clad in sweats and gathered along Howard Avenue.

"As-salaamu'alaikum, brothers," he greeted them.

"Wa'alaikum as-salaam," he heard in a chorus of response.

Once Tawfiq—one of the oldest among them—appeared, the imam led the pack on a jog around and around the blocks surrounding Howard. They passed the same brick buildings looming overhead, the same line of cars parked by the curbsides, and the same groups of kids playing on the sidewalk. My father felt eyes from the apartments above watching him and could almost hear the chuckles he imagined were directed at him and the rest of the group for participating in such a redundant activity. But the goal wasn't to travel a certain distance; rather, it was to jog nonstop for one hour.

"That's what's wrong with us: We specialize in everything short," Tawfiq said as he ran, noting several African Americans known as the world's greatest sprinters, people like the Olympians Jesse Owens, Wilma Rudolph, Tommie Smith, and John Carlos. Meanwhile, Kenyans, Ethiopians, and other Africans won marathons.

"We need to develop a long-distance mentality," Tawfiq told the brothers flanking him, perhaps preparing them for how long it would take to grow their tiny Muslim mosque into a substantial religious movement.

Tawfiq had set everyone's expectations high. They may have been worshipping in Bedford-Stuyvesant at a masjid that doubled as the imam's studio apartment, but he said MIB would grow to become so much more. It would have its own mosque building. It would run its own businesses. It would create an "indigenous Muslim intelligentsia" of homegrown black Muslims possessing their own culture and customs based in Harlem.

This was everything my father wanted to hear. He was anxious for MIB to become a force within the black community. He envisioned satellite MIB mosques opening in cities all around the country and MIB's growing so large that it rivaled the Nation of Islam with dozens of businesses and many thousands of members. He dreamed about Black Nationalism in action and anticipated the righteousness of Islam uplifting black folks nationwide.

My father watched Tawfiq push ahead, as he would often do during these jogs. The distance did not challenge him, so sometimes he turned around and ran part of the way backward. He faced the brothers as he lectured them about the mosque's possibilities. Other times, he weighted his ankles, forcing his legs to achieve greater buoyancy or else suffer greater damage when his feet crashed down into pavement. Tawfiq seemed possessed with an irrepressible strength that made evident why he was imam and chosen to lead. But he never ran off on his own—everyone stayed together. If someone fell back, another brother had to slow down and help him catch up with the rest of the group. No one got left behind.

My father kept up well on this first run. Although winded by the end of the hour, when the group returned to Tawfiq's building he felt ready for whatever would follow. He and the other brothers filed into the studio apartment and arranged themselves into a circle so that all the men could see one another. My father noticed some tall, some short. Some had been athletes before, some hadn't. Some were ready for Tawfiq's challenge, others were not.

"We'll begin with squats," Tawfiq said.

With their hands atop their heads, elbows out, legs shoulder-width apart, and toes pointing forward, the brothers bent at the knees while leaning their chests toward their thighs then, stood straight up again. And repeat. It was like a vertical crunch.

I can do this, my father told himself. And repeat. And repeat. The goal was to do one thousand squats without stopping, Tawfiq said. Each man was to start with just thirty-five and, every Saturday, work his way up by five. And repeat. And repeat. And repeat.

Actually being fit enough to complete one thousand squats wasn't the most important point of the exercise to Tawfiq. He was drilling the brothers on consistency and setting long-term goals. To sustain themselves as Muslims, who were required to perform five prayers a day, every day, no matter where they were or what they were doing when the adhan was called, they would need that consistency. And to build the kind of Muslim community Tawfiq had in mind, he'd need brothers in it for the long haul. He was planning a marathon, not a sprint.

Once my father completed his introductory thirty-five squats, he felt good, so he decided he would show the brothers he could go the distance by doing more, and more. After a while, his energy began to wane and he wanted to stop. Some of the other brothers did, dropping out of the circle at their appointed number for the week. But my father thought, *I can do more*, so he pushed himself to keep going.

Soon, the air in the small studio was thick with the body heat of determined brothers. The ones left who were slightly older seemed to be doing just as well as those around my father's age, and the imam didn't appear tired at all. My father couldn't allow himself to give up. He'd been his eighth grade class's runner-up for Mr. Physical Fitness 1964, after all.

And he was a Kushite. Repeat. Repeat. But his thighs ached, his head was cloudy, and sweat slipped down his forehead in torrents. Facing his brothers, he told himself, *I can't let any of them outdo me.* Repeat.

My father kept squatting for a long time, spurred on by competitiveness, determination, and fear of embarrassment.

Then, sometime around the five hundredth squat, he could do no more. Kushite or not, he had to stop. He excused himself from the circle and made his way to the bathroom, where he promptly vomited with all the strength he had left.

22

Club for Believers

WHILE I WAS IN HIGH SCHOOL, folding tables lined concrete curbsides like a path of dominoes along Harlem's 125th Street from about the boulevard named for Malcolm X to the one called Frederick Douglass. Mostly straight, the path sometimes jutted into side streets only to stop abruptly and pick back up on the next block of 125th, steady and uninterrupted until reaching its eventual end. The tabletops, often made three-dimensional with a propped-up wire rack or velvet board displaying the most eye-catching of goods, were largely flattened boutiques packed with books, toys, T-shirts, purses, wood carvings, straw baskets, incense and oils, African fabrics, handmade jewelry, and caps in summer or hats, gloves, and scarves in winter.

My mother and I used to frequent these vendors, the ebony-toned faces of our favorites—from Senegal, Côte d'Ivoire, and Gambia, they told us—and their customary spots along the route becoming more familiar with each weekend trip.

Then, one day when I was fifteen, Ummi told me that the vendors would no longer be allowed to line Harlem's curbs, tempting passersby with their wares. Instead, they were being forced into a communal vending area on 116th Street, farther from the Triborough Bridge that deposited us from Long Island onto 125th Street and distant from normal pedestrian traffic. It had something to do with Mayor Giuliani's wanting to clean up the city and rid it of "illegal street vending." *Whatever*, I thought. To me, it had everything to do with his wanting to slight black people and keep us out of sight.

I envisioned the new location as an indoor flea market, possibly warmer in the winter months but decidedly less fun than trolling Harlem's main thoroughfare, taking in its sights, sounds, and smells while shopping for goodies. After hearing about the change, Ummi and I drove uptown that December, partly to pick up Kwanzaa supplies for our 1994 celebration and partly to see the new quarters of our beloved vendors.

The 116th Street market wasn't actually inside a building. Called an open-air market, it was between two buildings, on a square patch of asphalt, beneath a large white tent held up by metal bars. It was cold, secluded, and monotonous. No more than half the vendors we usually saw had made the move there. Missing, too, was the backdrop of Harlem— the hip-hop blaring from car stereos, the stores with propped-open doors beckoning passersby to come inside, the roasted nuts sold from metal carts to munch while we shopped. All gone. The atmosphere that had made such a trip worthwhile was gone.

This sucks, I thought, as we mazed through the tight corridors the vendors had formed with their folding tables, covered with white waterproof cloth. The space was too small. Customers crowded the booths. I couldn't see what I wanted and I didn't like to wait. Nevertheless, Ummi and I trawled the aisles—she, searching for a new kinara so we could stop using the one Abi had carved when we began celebrating the holiday together some five years earlier, and I, on the lookout for unique, quality handmade jewelry.

Ummi didn't wear much jewelry, but she had two of the coolest rings I had ever seen stashed in a burgundy velvet pouch in her underwear drawer. One was an unusually thick gold engagement ring with a small diamond set simply in its center. It had belonged to Grandma Louise, but after she and Grandpa Bob divorced, she gave it to Abi to give to Ummi. The other was a gold band about a third of an inch wide with Arabic script swirling around the center that read, "Bismillah, al-rahman al-rahim." It was Ummi's wedding band.

I wanted both rings but had no use for an engagement ring and didn't want the stigma of wearing the wedding band of a never-married divorced couple. Besides, Ummi's fingers were slenderer than mine. While her band was too big for my pinky, I couldn't manage to squeeze it onto my ring finger.

The 116th Street market, though unimpressive, had quite a few ring sellers. The style then was sterling silver of different designs; many were curved like a rippling wave, others featured an ankh or an amber or onyx stone. Others were just a simple circlet. Although I had already written the place off and was only dragging my feet through the aisles to keep up with Ummi, I discovered a tray of rings at one booth that included a single row topped with the prominent contour of a star and crescent; I knew the combination to be a symbol of Islam.

At home, I had a book Abi had bought me of black-and-white photographs of Malcolm X, and in most I spotted what looked like a thick gold or silver class ring on his left ring finger. But in place of a precious stone mounted in the center, there was a dark circle embossed with a shiny star and crescent. It looked like the type of ring that could be pressed into wax to make a distinctive stamp for sealing envelopes. Or the type awarded for winning a championship game. It was the type of ring given to members of an exclusive club. His was the club to which I already felt I belonged—one for believers; getting the ring would just make it official.

"How much is that ring?" I asked the vendor, pointing to a row of them, all identical in sterling silver, but more elegant and feminine than the one Malcolm X wore. From one side, a three-dimensional star shot up over the finger, and from the other, a crescent moon opened wide, threatening to overtake the sparkler but never coming close enough to touch it. As in nature, the two hovered in perfect harmony.

"Those? Are for men," he said.

"They are?" I asked, chuckling and reaching for the one I'd tried on while the vendor was busy helping another customer. I took off my glove. "It fits my finger," I said, showing him how natural it looked on my hand.

The man, whose midnight skin contrasted sharply with the plain white cloth kufi on his head, wore something like a blanket draped over his shoulders to keep warm. He was no taller than I and, when not attending to customers, sat on a small stepladder behind the L formed by his two corner tables. Standing, he glanced down at my outstretched hand and annoyed but apparently satisfied, begrudgingly named his price.

The amount was more than the ten dollars I usually paid for a pair of earrings or the fifteen I paid for two pairs; it was more than I was willing to pay for a beaded choker, fifteen dollars; a lanyard bracelet, five; scented oil, two to five dollars; or any other trinket I had bought on 125th Street before. But this was no simple trinket. More than the interchangeable earrings I always wore or even an attractive bracelet I knew no one else would have, the ring said something about me. It spoke to who I was increasingly defining myself to be. It might have been a quiet statement, but it was at just the volume I needed.

I handed over the money.

Immediately, I began wearing my ring on the fourth finger of my right hand every day. I was saving my left ring finger for an engagement ring and, later, a wedding band. But having a symbol of my beliefs opposite where my wedding ring would someday be made me feel as though I had entered into some sort of sacred union with Allah. I could not actually be wedded to Him, but symbolically, I was committed.

Soon, people on the street, at checkout counters, and in take-out restaurants who didn't know me but saw the ring on my hand began to ask if I was Muslim.

"Yes," I would answer.

"As-salaamu'alaikum," they'd say smiling.

I'd grin and return the hello: "Wa'alaikum as-salaam." No stranger had ever offered me salaams before. With my uncovered hair and clothing that only adhered to my personal definition of modesty, no one had been able to tell just by looking at me that I was Muslim. When these greetings came, I felt filled with the warmth of recognition and the embrace of acceptance.

Yet at the same time, insecurity took hold as I began wondering whether the person who greeted me was asking himself why I didn't look more Muslim: Where was my khimar? Why wasn't I properly covered? Why did it take a ring for him to be able to tell what I was?

I felt like a fraud. Just as if I'd gone back to the time my sister confronted me about our parents not being married, I felt illegitimate. Again. Sure, I said that I was Muslim confidently, even proudly, but I still wasn't quite sure what being Muslim meant. Who was I to claim it?

Though in my heart I was a believer—I was Muslim—in practice I knew I probably wasn't. I wanted to know for sure.

23

Thanksgiving

MY GRANDFATHER HADN'T gotten over the disappointment of my father's leaving college without a degree before he showed up at his house in Teaneck one day with a beard, wearing a kameez and kufi, toting a prayer rug, and calling himself a Muslim named Hasan. It appeared as though my father had not only rejected the higher education his father had tried to provide but also the religion my grandfather had raised him in and even the name—his own name—my grandfather had given him. My grandfather was angry.

"I gave that boy everything. Everything he ever wanted," he told his wife, Vivian. "I got him a dog. Bought him a car. I sent the boy to school. I paved the way for him. And now look, he just turns his goddamn back on us. What the hell is wrong with him?"

Add to all that: within a year of becoming Muslim, my father had met and married a young woman from his mosque and had a son with her. My father was under no illusion about his father's displeasure. Nevertheless, my grandfather had invited him over for Thanksgiving and my father accepted.

"I would appreciate it if you didn't put any pork in the food or use any pork products while you're cooking," my father requested, aware of my grandfather's kitchen habits. "Muslims don't eat pork, and I want to be able to enjoy the meal."

There was a loud sigh on the other end of the phone. "All right, all right. I won't use any pork. Just come on to the dinner," my grandfather growled.

The day arrived and my father showed up dressed in the style Imam Tawfiq had prescribed for MIB brothers: a kameez that hovered around the knees, dress pants, shined shoes, and a head covering—as the Prophet Muhammad wore—that day, a crocheted kufi. My father had not only changed his name and dress to become Muslim, his commitment manifested in numerous other ways: He would make salat on a subway platform if it was time for one of the five daily prayers; his Qur'anic study had evolved from reading for knowledge to reading for pleasure; and in addition to fasting for Ramadan, he also cut food and drink during daylight hours at random other times, whenever he felt compelled to strengthen his discipline. But that Thanksgiving, he wasn't fasting. There was quite a spread before him: a huge turkey, mounds of stuffing, gooey gobs of macaroni and cheese, a slick mountain of collard greens, piles of picture-perfect corn muffins, chunks of syrupy candied yams, and more. The sweet aroma of the yams mixed with the smokiness of the greens, making my father's belly grumble.

It would have been so easy for my grandfather to just drop a pork neck into the pot of greens, stir it up, and have no one be the wiser. My father, knowing this, eyed the food suspiciously. But when nothing looked or smelled amiss, he filled his plate, cupped his hands in front of his face for a du'a, and began to eat.

Everything was delicious, as my father knew it would be. He'd missed my grandfather's cooking. Then, after eating halfway through his corn muffin, my father noticed something strange.

"Hey, Dad, what is this pink in this corn muffin?" he asked, staring at the spongy yellow mass as if it were a kitten that had just sprouted a second head.

"Aww, don't worry about it, Robbie. I didn't put pork in anything," my grandfather said, reassuring my father about the flecks of pink. "That ain't nothing but some ham."

My father dropped the corn muffin. "Come on, Dad. I asked you—"

"You grew up eating this, so what you mean? I fixed this food and you gonna eat it. Hell with what they telling you not to eat."

My grandfather's reluctance to accept my father's new way of life didn't exactly encourage my father to do what he did next. My father simply had no other option. He gathered up the nerve to head back out to Teaneck and sit my grandfather down.

"Dad, I have an idea for a new business I want to start: a tearoom," he said.

"What in the hell is a tearoom?"

My father had heard about them from Imam Tawfiq, who'd studied Arabic and Islamic jurisprudence at Cairo's Al-Azhar University and frequented tearooms there. In a calm tone and deliberate pace, my father began explaining the concept—the café, the teas, the pastries; the mosque, the Muslims, their morals. Before my grandfather had a chance to doubt that this tearoom could actually net money, my father laid out a brief overview of the business plan. He talked about revenue streams, wholesale suppliers, and the lack of a need for payroll. He'd prepared answers for every question he could foresee his father asking—and even some he couldn't—because he knew my grandfather wouldn't agree to anything without giving him the third degree.

This was the way my grandfather dealt with any proposition, including my father's decision to become Muslim, which is why he kept his intentions secret until he'd already converted.

"All right. So where do you plan on opening this tearoom?" his father asked.

That was the question my father had been waiting for. "I found the perfect place," he said, a smile coming over his face. "Come on. I'll show you." The two of them got in my father's car and began traversing roads familiar to them both. First, they left from their block in Teaneck, where my grandfather had once armed himself with an ornamental doorknob in one hand and the leash of my father's Collie, Champ, in the other to protect my father and his friends from a group of neighborhood boys who threatened to beat them up. Next, they drove through the tunnel that connected New Jersey to New York—and separated who my father was from who he wanted to be and was now becoming. Finally, they arrived at my grandfather's old block on Sugar Hill, where my father first sought to meld the bond with my grandfather that his indiscretions had torn asunder.

"Here it is," my father said, walking my grandfather up a patterned iron staircase painted black. A "for lease" sign was stuck in the picture window. They shaded their eyes with their hands and pressed them to the glass around the sign to get a glimpse of the space inside. My father described a possible floor plan. Then, turning, they faced the traffic of 145th Street and Hillview Towers, the building that had represented change for them both.

My grandfather, again tickled by how my father's exploits forced him to revisit the times and circumstances of his own life, eased into a better mood. "It's a good location. We had a lot of good times over here," he said.

"Uh-huh, we did. So what do you think? Can I have the money to start my business?" My father, expecting a high bar to clear, didn't realize that this time was different. My grandfather had incentive to lend him the money. Despite having a new wife and young son to provide for, my father was ill equipped for his responsibilities as a provider. He might've been co-owner of an incense shop with his best friend Abdul-Malik, working as a street vendor, and the former manager of the mosque's first business, a health food store, but he was barely piecing together a living. He didn't have a degree or what my grandfather considered a "real job" and had no prospects.

My grandfather knew my father needed significant work that would pay him a substantial income just for his burgeoning family to survive. Finally, with this business idea, he was thinking along the right lines.

"All right, Robbie. I'll give you the money," my grandfather said, committing to provide my father with the month's rent and month's security needed to open the tearoom. "But make this thing work."

My father, envisioning plans for the homegrown Muslim enterprise that silhouetted his mind starting to take shape, said, "I will, Dad, insha'Allah."

24

America, the Beautiful

MY MOTHER HAD COME OVER to Abi's house to pick Muhammad and me up after school. She would usually knock on the door, tell us to come on, then return to the car to wait, but this time she stayed on the stoop. It was a chilly evening. The sun had set and stars were beginning to twinkle in a ripening blueberry-hued sky.

"Hi, Hassan," Ummi said, her tone serious and flat. I gathered my things to leave, but she stopped me. "Wait a minute, Feeya. I need to talk to your father," she said, still standing in the doorway but refusing to cross the threshold and make herself comfortable in what had become my father's house ever again.

I heard her mention the name Salim. He was the son of one of my mother's three best friends, Haniya (Weekly), I'd learned recently. I was familiar with her three children who lived with her, all of them younger than me. But I had never heard of Salim or even known that Umti Haniya had a son four years older than me until I met him at her apartment in the Bronx a couple of months earlier.

Apparently, he and his younger brother, Haniya's next oldest son, whom I'd also never known, had spent years living with their father, Abdul-Malik, in Africa. Not by choice. After he and Haniya split up, Abdul-Malik, who himself had grown up on Manhattan's Lower East Side, had decided that 1980s New York City at the advent of the crack era, with a mother he judged too steeped in the dunya, was not the best environment in which to raise Muslim children. He thought their sons, then around eight and six years old, would fare better with him and his new wife in Gambia. So he took them and kept them there, away from their mother. And now, after maybe a dozen years apart, Salim had chosen to return to America and to his mother.

I had imagined their reunion like the final scene in *The Color Purple*: the once-American son turned "African," overjoyed to see his small, quaint mother, but now larger than her, more worldly, no longer able to even speak her language.

My mother had brought my sister and me to Haniya's one warm day to meet this strange African son for ourselves. We drove to the Bronx, to her building. I remember walking up stairs to get to Haniya's apartment, and after my mother knocked on her painted black door but before Umti Haniya could answer it, I spotted a young man in a white-and-scarlet striped T-shirt tiptoeing behind us in the hallway. He looked at me and put a finger to his lips so I would not give him away. Then he leaned close to my mother's ear and in a low tone said, "Hi, Umti Labiba," surprising her. Ummi spun around and burst into one of her most gleeful laughs, wrapping her arms around Salim's neck as if she too hadn't seen him in more than a decade, even though she was the one who'd driven his mother to JFK to pick him up after his flight from Gambia some months earlier. He beamed as they hugged, my mother rocking him side to side, and I knew I liked him already.

Once Ummi released him from her embrace and I could get a good look at Salim, I liked him even more. He was undoubtedly American— a New Yorker even—with style and an air of self-confidence that emanated from the tips of the tiny twists sprouting like a Koosh ball off his head and through the pores of his skin, rich and deep like wild blackberries raining from low-slung canes. This spirit radiated from his gaze, dancing with kindness and yet steady with focus, to the warmth in his straight-toothed smile, reflecting both his capacity for joy and his ability to inspire it in others. Salim, I decided, was beautiful.

Bewildered by it, all I could manage to say to greet him was, "As-salaamu'alaikum."

"Wa'alaikum as-salaam," he returned, still smiling, almost laughing at my formality.

After a moment, Umti Haniya opened her door, greeted us with her high-pitched cheer, and we all went inside.

And now my mother was telling Abi that Salim was dead.

"He's been killed, shot," she said. He'd only been in America for nine months, and just like that, he was gone.

Apparently, his mere presence had managed to stir up resentment among some young men around his age that he was acquainted with. There might have been a dispute over a girl, or maybe some feelings of jealousy over all the attention Salim got when he returned. No one could pinpoint for me the exact reason why anyone would have wanted to kill him, but one day, another young black man had shot him dead.

"Why didn't you tell me that he was in danger?" my father asked my mother upon hearing the news. He sounded angry, but also hurt, as if something in him had broken. The hurt, no doubt, came from outside, from a world that continually put black men in danger, from a society that labeled them as the danger. But the anger, as before, was directed inside, at my mother. Abi started walking away from her at the front door but then stopped. "He could've come out here and stayed with me," he offered, too late.

I was just learning that Abi had a connection to Salim as well. Salim's father, Abdul-Malik, had been Abi's best friend back when they all—Ummi, Abi, Haniya, and Abdul-Malik—had been in the mosque, MIB, together. Although Abi hadn't been in contact with Abdul-Malik since he'd left for Gambia, their friendship went back twenty-five years. They would all be reunited at Salim's funeral.

Ummi, Aliya, and I drove back to the Bronx for his viewing. It was held in a tiny room in a funeral home, too small to contain all the grief that soon engulfed it. We found seats among several narrow rows of folding chairs and sat just long enough to brace ourselves. Then the three of us stood, linked hands, and pulled each other toward the front of the room to Salim's coffin.

Ummi squeezed my hand too hard, the way she often did to get a reaction from me whenever we took a picture together. That time, I knew she couldn't help herself. Salim was born just the year after Aliya, both Haniya's and Ummi's first children. They had seen him grow from baby to little boy and, after some time away, young man. Yet there he lay before us, dead at only nineteen.

Reluctantly, I peeked into the coffin then couldn't look away. Salim's body—wrapped in the Muslim tradition for burial—was wound tight like a chrysalis in white sheets, layer upon layer, overlapping and tucked under, narrow around the feet and wide at the elbows, revealing nothing but a tuft of his carefree mass of twists and his handsome brown face. His skin was the color of a cocoa bean rubbed smooth with careful fingers. His eyebrows were bushy and dark. His eyelashes long like cat whiskers. His lips perfectly defined. Despite his ugly murder, I still recognized him as one of the beautiful ones.

When we saw his mother, she gave us each a lingering hug. She smiled blankly as she wrapped her bony arms around me. Then she released my body, looking at me and through me at the same time. I don't think she even knew it was me she was hugging. She was standing right in front of me but was so far away.

I felt as if I'd always known Umti Haniya, a thin woman with narrow eyes, skin the color of fox fur, and that girlish voice. Ummi told me they'd met through their husbands, who used to run a teahouse in Harlem together for the mosque, and quickly became close. Ummi and Haniya remained friends after Abdul-Malik left for Africa and after Ummi and Abi split up, and during all that time, I'd come to know her a little too.

Of all my siblings, I was sure I was Umti Haniya's favorite. As with most adults who knew us, she was most impressed and amused by Aliya's outspokenness and sense of humor, but it was clear that she and I were kindred spirits. We both embraced a nerdy quirkiness that earned us a certain degree of ridicule from those less enthusiastic about anthropological or spiritual interests. If I happened to answer the phone when she called, we might talk for a few minutes about museums or our latest writing projects before she asked to speak to my mother. Before heading to the viewing that day, although I desperately wished I didn't have to go, I thought my presence might comfort Umti Haniya in some small way. Seeing her, I knew that notion had been naïve.

We sat back down, and the viewing continued with more and more people—Abi and Abdul-Malik included—streaming past Salim's body. Eventually, Haniya could no longer hold herself together. She broke down sobbing, her body limply folding onto itself as she heaved loud wails. Ummi and Aliya, still weeping and sitting on either side of me, both squeezed my hands then, no doubt resonating with the profundity of Umti Haniya's loss.

But how could it have happened, I wondered? I understood the circumstances of Salim's murder, but I couldn't comprehend—or didn't want to acknowledge—how such a young man with a life full of promise could be so senselessly killed.

As I'd gathered from conversations with Ummi and Abi over the years, Islam was supposed to give our lives purpose. It was supposed to keep Salim, and all of us children, away from danger. It was supposed to protect us from the ills of inner-city life. That's part of the reason our parents, who themselves grew up amid tough times in Harlem and the Bronx, had become Muslims, wasn't it? Through the morally upright lifestyle that Islam promotes and they adopted, they wanted to transform themselves so they could instill in us the principles and the consciousness for a better life. Through Islam, they wanted us to strive for something more than what they'd had. Through Islam, they wanted us to be wiser. Through Islam, they wanted us to be more righteous. With Islam, they believed we would be safe.

Gazing at Salim's body and listening to the cacophony of cries it conjured, I knew that notion too had been naïve. It seemed Islam could accomplish none of that. Or maybe Islam could make black people's lives better, as long as they were in a different environment. In Gambia, he seemed safe. In the Bronx, Muslim or not, he was just another black man shot dead. So if Islam could not protect us, what was the point of our parents converting, making their own and our lives more complicated with Islam's many rules and edicts? What would be the point of going to a mosque every week? What would be the point of praying five times a day? What was the point of it all, I wondered?

But I knew there had to be a point to Salim's death. Ummi had taught me that while man can plan, Allah is the best of planners. Surely this too was part of His plan; it was His will. I just couldn't figure out what message Allah was trying to send with it.

As I racked my brain, sorrowful outbursts soon punctuated my every thought and reverberated through my slightest movement.

If he had only stayed in Africa, I thought. Grasping Ummi and Aliya's hands tighter, I attempted to let them know that I—who was supposed to be unaffected because I had met Salim just once—was there for them.

But I could not be the strong one. The bawling in the funeral home had become so profound, it drowned every single other sound out. Finally, my mother, steadily wiping tears from her face, and my sister, intermittently whimpering in my ear, broke my resolve not to be sucked into the vortex of sorrow steadily overtaking the room.

25

Muslim, or Not?

IT WAS A FRIGID WINTER DAY. Wind whipped around my stockinged legs as I stood in the cemetery near our old home. The long rectangular plot was grassy, flat, and treeless, as lifeless and unremarkable as one would think a cemetery should be. A firefighters' training school sat across the street, its blaring sirens, raging fires, and torrents of water repeatedly failing to wake the dead. I'd ridden past this gravesite countless times gazing at the slate and gray, tall and taller-still headstones, never once thinking I'd enter its gates or be there to bury one so young. Twenty-four. Just twenty-four birthdays, and he would have no more. On three, four, or maybe five of them we spoke. He was the one who'd started calling me.

"Feeya! Come to the phone! It's for you!" my mother shouted from downstairs one afternoon. "Feeya!"

Leery, because no one ever called for me, I bounded down the stairs but only tentatively reached for the phone that felt like an extension of my mother—her shoulder always raised to prop it into place, her ear always glued to catch news from its earpiece—and held it to my ear.

"Hello?" I didn't see why whomever my mother was talking to couldn't just pass the message through her.

"Happy birthday, Feeya," a male voice said from the other end.

"Oh, thank you," I smiled, remembering it was my birthday.

"Do you know who this is?"

It had to be a relative or someone I knew through my family because teachers and classmates were the only ones who called me by my whole name, "Sufiya." But I didn't recognize the voice. "No," I said.

"It's Khuz. Trenedia's brother."

He didn't have to add that last part. Trenedia might have come to mind easily as my sister's friend, but I didn't know any other Khuz— and still don't. His whole name, Khuzaymah, stood out in my memory because it was the most Muslim-sounding name of any of the Muslims I knew. Only my brother Isa's middle name, Al-Muwahid, sounded slightly more like it would only be uttered in a Jeddan bazaar or on a sand dune of the Arabian Desert (and for that, to his dismay, it was a never-ending source of our jokes). From what I heard, Khuz's parents had been part of the Nation of Islam at one point, then became Sunni Muslims, and by the time my mother met them and their kids when I was just a toddler, they too had abandoned their mosque and held a precarious relationship with Islam. My mother and Khuz's mother hit it off.

"Oh hi, Khuz. Happy birthday to you, too." I remembered then that we shared the same birthday, but he bested me by eight years. He must've been turning seventeen, eighteen, or nineteen that first time he called. I blushed at the thought of a teenager, and a boy at that, thinking a little girl like me worthy of celebrating on her birthday. But Khuz wasn't that kind of boy. He was slender, at least six feet tall, with a coffee-bean complexion, a thick halfro like *Reading Rainbow*'s Levar Burton, and a classically handsome face. Yet, though he was the oldest of his trio of siblings, he was decidedly not their tough protector. He was introverted, sensitive, and a bit of a loner, all like me. I wondered whether everyone with our birthday had the same personality.

"So, what are you up to today?" he asked, beginning our birthday tradition of calling each other with well wishes. Even if no one else cared to honor our birth, we would do that for each other, we water signs, we crabs. But no more.

No one would tell me the cause of Khuz's death. No one wanted to talk about it. Their silence alone told me more than I should have known. Maybe it wasn't intentional, I allowed, just an unfortunate accident. Without confirmation, I was left to think that maybe his (our) sensitivity had something to do with it, or his (our) differences, or his (our) sensitivity about his (our) differences. I was left to think that maybe the same, by the time I turned twenty-four, would become of me.

The man officiating Khuz's funeral, just months after I'd attended Salim's, called me out of my reverie.

"At this point in time, we're going to pray salat al-janazah. Would all the Muslims please step forward?" he asked.

Suddenly, I didn't know what to do. *Am I Muslim or not?* I asked myself.

It was a simple question. But the man's request felt more like a test to determine if I could square my identity—who I believed I was in private—with who I showed myself to be in public. *Am I Muslim or not?*

Had Khuz—Khuzaymah, owner of the most Islamic-sounding first name I'd known and yet, contrary to the masculinity epitomized by the man who inspired scores to Islam, "our own black shining prince" Malcolm, was a man only about as rough as silk on skin—been made to question himself in this way too? Was he Muslim, or not?

People started to separate themselves. My eyes scanned the mumbling group of mourners beginning to line up behind the long casket that held Khuz's frame. I noticed lots of black folks, some wearing kufis and khimars, but some bare-headed as I was beneath the upturned hood of my wool coat. They were converts raising their kids in the lingering shadow of the post–civil rights, Black Muslim movement. They were members of the second generation, who learned from their parents about Islam's glory mainly in retrospect. But they were all Muslim. If they were, why couldn't I be? I asked myself. Nobody there would question whether I belonged with them or not, I realized, because everybody there was just like me.

Of course, I'm Muslim, I told myself, reassured. Quickly, I joined the line of women stretched taut and wide like an unstrummed guitar string, until we all touched shoulder-to-shoulder. Once in position, nobody moved.

"Takbir!" the man leading the services suddenly shouted.

Startled and confused by his unexpected outburst, I said nothing while the voices of the rest of the group rose in unison: "Allahu akbar."

Everyone's hands then crossed over their torsos before they began to pray.

I recognized the prayer as the same one I once sang with my family huddled close, the same I'd begun to forget when Abi cast us from his house. It was the same that the film *Malcolm X* had reminded me that I loved and that I now recited alone whenever I needed to talk to God. Hurriedly, I embraced myself and took pride that this time, I knew just what to do.

"*Alhamdulillahi rabbi-il al-amin . . .*," I joined the other Muslims.

The prayer ended and the man up front again shouted "Takbir!"

But I picked up on that one too late too and fell silent when everyone else intoned, "Allahu akbar," God is the greatest. I told myself I would not miss the call and response if it happened again.

Next, the man up front delivered a short burst of Arabic I did not recognize and could barely hear.

I—and everyone else this time—remained silent.

He yelled a third takbir, to which I finally knew to respond, "Allahu akbar."

But as the group shifted to offering a du'a for Khuz, I no longer knew the Arabic words I was supposed to say. My lessons with Abi had not gone far beyond the alphabet and a few basic words and phrases. Embarrassed that I did not know how to adequately honor Khuz or properly pay my respects to Salim when he passed, I could only watch the woolen coat–clad backs of the mourners who continued the prayer before me while I stood by, mute.

My silence, however, was quickly overcome by the din of questions about my faith clamoring in my mind. The questions had been there for years by then, accumulating with every Friday I did not worship at a mosque, each khutbah I did not hear, and every wave of my mother or father's hand dismissing me when I approached with a religious concern. The questions had waited patiently for an opportune time and an accommodating answerer to be asked, but they could not wait any longer. I needed to know why I hadn't been taught the funeral prayer; why I hadn't been raised to cover myself; why I hadn't been told that even if I was oblivious to what was halal and what was haram, every other Muslim knew and would spurn me for being ignorant of the rules of good and bad.

I was ashamed of my ignorance. I had to do something to dispel it.

After leaving my sister to be with her friend, I sat in my mother's car and started asking her my questions on our way home.

"Do Muslims believe in an afterlife?" I blurted into the silence, concerned about what might happen to Khuz's soul.

"Well, yes. We believe that after you die, if you lived a righteous life, your spirit lives on in Paradise," Ummi answered in a measured tone.

"Um-hum. What about reincarnation?"

"Hmm, I think that's more of a Hindu thing."

"OK. Then, what is Paradise?" I continued down my mental checklist of all I'd been wondering about.

"It's Heaven," she said, her tone harsher, more pointed.

Undeterred, I persisted: "Well, what's it like? Are there, like, pearly gates and stuff like that? What about angels?"

"Feeya, I don't know. I haven't been there. Why don't you look it up? What are all these questions for anyway?"

"Because I want to know," I said. "If I call myself a Muslim, then I should know what Muslims believe." To me, that answer was obvious. "I mean, I didn't even know the prayer, Ummi."

"What prayer?"

"At the cemetery."

"Oh, that? Nobody knows it."

"Well, people were saying it," I countered.

"Yeah, you just stand up there with them and let them say it. Nobody knows you didn't know it."

That wasn't good enough for me. I challenged my mother directly: "How come you didn't teach me?"

She sighed. "Come on, Feeya."

"What? How come?"

And then her tone turned sharp: "You know who you should ask? Your father. He'd probably have a lot to say on the subject."

I knew what that meant: My mother wanted me to leave her alone because she did not want to talk about Islam anymore, maybe not ever. She had just watched another of her friends bury her firstborn; she was not in the mood for my interrogation of Islam.

But what I learned from Abi, his penchant for dominating Ummi and showing her little respect, had by then become the family business. It was passed down first to Aliya, who had taken to frequent bitter arguments with my mother, and was now taken up by sixteen-year-old me. I took newfound liberty in showing my disdain for how much of a pushover I thought my mother had been as my father's wife and at what I felt she had sacrificed by not standing up for herself sooner. At the same time, my mother, at age forty, took fresh pleasure in showing me she was no pushover.

I rolled my eyes at her suggestion; we both knew Ummi often grew silent when I tried to bring up Islam. She had been stuck in a painful "marriage" that wouldn't have happened without Islam; I understood that, but for the most part I didn't care. I only wanted the facts. I didn't see anything wrong with that. So I pressed on: "But Abi's not here, Ummi. You are."

"Hmmm, and that tells you something, doesn't it?"

"What?" I asked, questioning the logic of her statement rather than seeking an answer to it. I could see that the conversation was quickly turning into an argument, one I didn't care to engage in. I hissed out a sigh, turned my head, and gazed out the window, ignoring my mother and that her friend's son's death and my questions had put her on edge, for the rest of our ride home.

————————————

One afternoon some months later, my mother called me to her room. It was spring, and a spirit of renewal permeated the air like the gush of a breeze off an ocean current. Ummi, Muhammad, and I had spent the past year settling into our new three-bedroom apartment in Freeport. It was a step up from our two-bedroom in Hempstead, where Muhammad had slept on a foldout foam sofa in the foyer and called the walk-in closet that held his clothes, car posters, and bass guitar his room. Now, we could sit on our very own terrace and watch neighborhood kids drop their bikes in the dirt before they played; we could open a kitchen cabinet without roaches scurrying about. After moving three times in the past four years, it looked as if we had finally found someplace we wanted to stay. We were all in a better mood.

"I have something I want to give you," Ummi said, before pulling a chair into her walk-in closet. The closet wasn't exactly walkable anymore because of all the clothes, shoes, and bags my mother had amassed in the past year, but she centered the chair within a pile of them, stood on top, and raised herself up on her tippy-toes to reach a shelf near the ceiling.

I wondered what 1970s hand-me-down I had lucked into.

Atop a stack of shoeboxes and a photo album, I watched Ummi put her hands not on a pair of sandals or a shoulder bag but a thick book.

A couple of months earlier, not long after Khuz's burial, Ummi had given me a gift-wrapped book for Kwanzaa. I tore the wrapping paper, skeptical but hopeful about what it contained. When I saw the title, *A Muslim Primer*, I could not disguise my disappointment. A handbook about Islam, however well intentioned, wasn't exactly the Muslim wisdom I wanted my Muslim mother to share with me. From her, I'd hoped to glean some personal connection to the faith. I wanted to learn what led her as an American teen to adopt this foreign religion. I wanted to absorb her firsthand experience with the mosque where she and Abi both found faith and each other. Handing me a book felt like another way for my mother to avoid answering my questions or remembering what it increasingly seemed she only wanted to forget.

Now, I watched her lower the thick book from the tower, step down from the chair, and thrust it in my direction.

I held out both hands to receive it.

"Are your hands clean?" Ummi asked, pulling the book back close to her body.

"Why?"

"Your hands need to be clean. Go wash them."

I walked up the hall to the bathroom and quickly ran my hands under warm water, anticipating learning the reason for such ritual. After drying them, I returned to find Ummi still standing by the closet.

She handed me the book.

"This is the Qur'an that your father and I gave your grandfather when we got married," she said. There was a worn brown paper bag book cover on it like the kind Ummi showed me how to wrap my textbooks with when I was in elementary school. Inside, I could feel that the pages were thin like tissue paper. I opened the front cover and found an inscription in Abi's handwriting:

> In the name of Allah the Beneficent the Merciful. "Read in the name of thy Lord who created; He created man from a clot. Read and thy Lord is most Honourable, who taught to write with the pen, taught man what He knew not (96:1–5)."

> To, Our father with our love, from, Hasan and Labiba.

On the opposite page, Abi had translated his message into intricate and careful Arabic. Each line teemed with curves and slashes, dots and circles. Two words—written in blue ink that was fading into a hazy, dreamy purple—were darker than the rest, where Abi had corrected his mistakes. His effort to demonstrate his knowledge of the language and his commitment to the faith, however, was earnest; I could see that the Qur'an was special.

By giving it to me, I felt as though Ummi was admitting her surrender in a small yet pivotal battle. Somehow, I'd gotten the ice encasing my mother's heart, which used to beat for Islam, to begin to melt. I smiled slightly in celebration of a victory I hadn't realized I'd been fighting for.

After watching me read the note, Ummi snatched the Qur'an back and said: "You're not supposed to just touch it any old way. Your hands should be clean and you have to protect it from dirt and dust." She started removing the cover and revealed that beneath it, the hardback was pine green with gold Arabic calligraphy on the front. "Holy Qur'an" it read in English.

"This one is all beat up, so you should put your own cover on it. And your mind should be free from any impure thoughts when you're reading it. You can't pass gas either."

"What?" I asked, shocked that there were so many rules. "But what if you have to?"

"Then you put it down, go pass gas, make wudu to cleanse yourself, and then pick it up again. And when you're not reading it, you should store it in the highest place possible."

"Why?" I asked.

"You treat it with reverence because it is the word of Allah."

It sounded like a lot of unnecessary rigamarole just to find out what being Muslim was all about. But if following a few rules was part of the process, I could handle that. Especially because I saw that Ummi was trying to open herself up to sharing some of her history in Islam with me. This was what I had wanted all along. It was what I'd been looking for when I stared into the small squarish photographs in Ummi's old photo albums. This was what it felt like Ummi had boxed up and forgotten to unpack when we left Abi and moved to Uniondale and then Hempstead and then here. For this unpacking, this opening, this miracle, I wondered how much thanks I owed to Khuz, how much to Salim.

"Thanks, Ummi," I said.

"You're welcome, Feeya. Read it in good health."

Satisfied for the moment, I took the Qur'an back to my room and sat across my bed with my back to the wall. It was time to start studying. I said, "Bismillah," like Abi told me I should whenever I commenced an important task, swept my hands over my face, and started flipping through the pages.

Most were halfway filled with normal-sized text and below it, lines and lines of fine print: footnotes. The upper half of each page was divided in two parts too. In the left column was English and in the right, Arabic. The script was ornate and beautiful, but completely incomprehensible. I stuck to the English and the corresponding numbered footnotes.

The beginning chapter was appropriately titled, "Al-Fatihah: The Opening." I read the first verse: "In the name of Allah, the Beneficent, the Merciful. Praise be to Allah, the Lord of the worlds, The Beneficent, the Merciful, Master of the day of Requital . . ." Instantly, I recognized it as the prayer—my prayer. It was the same one I had once sung with my family huddled close; the one Abi had helped me translate before we all scattered to different homes; the one that, no matter where I was, connected me to Muslims everywhere.

"Al-Fatihah," I said to myself, momentarily marveling at the strength of my faith despite the dearth of my knowledge. "So that's what it's called."

26

Her Own Way

AT BANU-HILAL HERBAL TEA ROOM, my mother could sit down after her classes at City College, where she was a freshman in 1972, drink a cup of tea, eat a piece of gingerbread, and feel as if transported to a Muslim land. Brothers with scraggly beards and thigh-skimming thawbs sat at the tables around her, sipping their own tea, reading Qur'an, and chewing on miswak sticks. The aroma of incense wafted through the air; jazz music played in the background; Arabic phrases sprung from conversation. She enjoyed almost everything about being there.

Her favorite, though, was lounging at a table with a cup of tea centered before her and a plate with pastry set off to her right. She'd breathe in the flowery fragrances rising from the glass as she sipped, then try to guess the ingredients of the slice of cake or bread she bit into, carefully savoring each morsel as she chewed. My mother had loved baking ever since she was a girl standing by her mother's aproned side, watching her mix flour, sugar, butter, and waiting for a little batter to put in her own Easy-Bake Oven. The tearoom brought this to mind.

When she was there, she could also drift up to the storefront to admire handmade clothes adorning the glass display case. Her eyes examined the intricate patterns that multicolored yarns formed on kufis. Beside them, she studied men's kameezes: long, sleek, and just as elegant. With a good look, my mother could tell if the stitchwork on each kufi would keep its form after wear and whether the cut of each kameez formed the proper symmetry. She'd been sewing for years; first, making clothes for her dolls on a toy machine with swatches her grandmother brought home from her job at a dressmaking factory; then, moving on to the old sewing machine her father bought and showed her how to thread and operate to make clothes for herself. Lately, she'd begun asking for more yards of fabric as the outfits she made had become longer and looser; inspecting the pieces at the tearoom made her ponder her Singer and what Muslim-inspired garb she might try to sew next.

Yes, she liked the tearoom. Except that when Salahuddin, her boyfriend since high school, asked her to accompany him there to listen to lectures about Islam, his new religion, she refused. Just because he went to the tearoom didn't mean that she had to go with him, she said. It was the same thing she'd told him about becoming Muslim, which he'd done and told her she should too.

"I don't need to take shahada 'cause you took shahada," she countered. If she wanted to, she said, she'd become Muslim in her own way, in her own time.

My mother was born Joanna Frances Taylor in December 1954, the fourth and last child of her father, Wade Hampton Taylor Sr., an MTA subway conductor, and her mother, Vivian Wheeler Taylor, a New York City rent examiner. She was their only daughter. She was raised in the working-class Mill Brook Houses of the South Bronx where, in 1958, when they moved there, she and her family were among the new housing project's first occupants.

My mother, Jody, as she was called, was always under the watch of her three older brothers, Wade Jr., Kenny, and Jon. They took her to Sunday school, Wade and Kenny even teaching it for a while, and my mother sat rapt, listening to the lessons about God, Jesus, and spirituality. It seemed that every other day of her week was a lesson not in religion but in how to be a proper young lady.

Saturdays were for long drives to Yonkers for its better supermarket prices with her father behind the wheel or for subway rides downtown to Gimbels department store with her mother seated beside her. For the subway, her mother forced her to put on a dress.

"But Mom," she complained, dreading the fitted waist and fluffy skirt of the frock awaiting her, "why do I have to wear a dress just to get on the subway?"

"You always have to look presentable, Jody," her mother said, "because people are always watching you."

And sure enough, as they trawled Gimbels hosiery department, a salesperson eyed their movements. My grandmother—easily five foot ten, wearing a size 11W pump, a 16 dress, with a full shapely figure, a complexion like rich fertile earth, and the airs of a duchess—was hard to miss.

"Can I help you?" the salesperson asked.

"Oh, we're just looking," my grandmother responded kindly. She knew just what she wanted and where to find them. Round-the-Clock nylons were her favorite. She wore them, along with a dress, sometimes a jacket, a set of clip-on earrings, often a matching necklace, a pair of pumps—some leather, some patent leather, some with a buckle, and others with a flower, but always pumps—and a complementary purse, every day to her job at the Bronx Borough Rent Office, where she dealt with landlord-tenant disputes. Round-the-Clock nylons came in her color and were guaranteed to fit.

"This is a good price, Jody," my grandmother said, taking note of the sale. "I better stock up." She bought a dozen pairs of pantyhose that day, leaving no chance to be unprepared if she happened to one day get a run. This propriety and exacting sense of style was the same that my grandmother demanded of my mother.

Every morning while she got dressed for school, my mother came to anticipate the moment her mother would stick her head in her bedroom door, examine her outfit, and ask in an accusatory tone, "Is that what you're wearing?"

It always annoyed her.

Her biweekly hair appointments at Miss Lulene's, however, did not. The cigarette-smoking, wig-wearing, heavy-handed Miss Lulene was initially her grandmother's hairdresser, then her mother's, and, eventually, Miss Holland, an older hairdresser in the shop known for her gentler touch, became hers.

My mother's grandmother wore her rapidly graying hair short. That way, there was not much mussing and fussing to worry about each day as she worked as a domestic. Before moving to New York, my mother's nana had cooked, cleaned, and minded the children of a white family in Flanders, New Jersey. Nana's mother and grandmother actually did too. The three of them lived in a house that the white family had built for them on its property and swapped them out to do the domestic work like a human Newton's cradle.

My grandmother and great-aunt grew up there, befriending white children and baffling them with their differences. At six or seven years old, the daughter of the white family my mother's nana cooked and cleaned for became so enamored with my grandmother that the little girl thought she'd do her a favor. After the two had played together all day, when bath time came, the girl naïvely asked her father, "Could you please scrub the black off of Vivian?"

"My dear, that is the color of her skin. It will not come off," her father explained, and the little girl wailed, dismayed that there was no way to make her beloved black friend white.

My grandmother and her sister integrated Flanders's otherwise white elementary school in the early 1930s, although, at their mother's insistence, they left town before high school, when she expected the allure of curious white boys to become too great. The lessons my grandmother learned there about how to carry herself among whites—how to speak, how to dress as one of only a pair of representatives of the entire black race—stuck with her.

And so, when she went to Miss Lulene's, she got her dark hair that she never let grow beyond the nape of her neck perfectly coifed into big layered curls that framed her face. She wore it this way always. She even had a wig in the same style to wear on vacations when she couldn't get in to see Miss Lulene. Like everything else, my grandmother was meticulous about her hair and would not allow anyone to catch her looking unkempt; she felt she couldn't afford to.

At first, my mother took it as a point of pride that she was grown enough to go to a beauty parlor. Every other week while she was in junior high, she took the bus to Miss Lulene's to have her hair pressed and curled. And when she started high school in 1968, and her family moved out of the projects and into a three-bedroom co-op apartment near the Bronx's Grand Concourse, less than a mile away from Miss Lulene's, her biweekly visits continued.

Around the same time, though, my mother and her best friend, Denise, together in their new teenage independence, began exploring a world that was changing all around them. Just before high school, Martin Luther King Jr. and Bobby Kennedy had been assassinated. By freshman year, more than half a million US troops were in Vietnam, and my mother's two oldest brothers, Wade and Kenny, were elsewhere overseas, having been drafted into the military.

My mother and Denise began buying black books from The Tree of Life Bookstore on 125th Street and Lenox Avenue to teach themselves the things they knew their schools wouldn't. They shunned lessons on Shakespeare in favor of writing and performing their own revolutionary poetry. They raised their fists in Black Power salutes; they bought Angela Davis posters and red, black, and green buttons. And my mother began dating a black revolutionary-in-training named Nate whose Afro was as round and planetary as a globe, revolving her entire world on its axis.

Despite my grandmother's attempts to raise my mother in a bubble of prim propriety, everything about her environment—from public school days in the gritty and in parts poverty-stricken Bronx, to family trips into the still segregated South, then north into Canada, which had been a bastion of black freedom for years—reflected the truth of her times. My mother, at fifteen years old, felt that her neatly pressed and curled hairstyle no longer did.

"Here you go, Jody," her mother said one beauty parlor weekend in 1970, handing her some money. "Give that to Miss Lulene."

My mother closed her fingers around the dollars and stuffed them into her purse. Then she and Denise, instead of boarding the bus to Miss Lulene's, took the subway to the 135th Street YMCA, walked into the first-floor barbershop, and said, "We want to get Afros."

My mother leaned back in the shampoo chair and let water wash the effects of a biweekly straightening comb out of her tresses; she sat up and suffered through a blow-dryer tugging height and width into her locks; and finally settled into the barber's chair as he trimmed roundness and revolution about her head. When it was done, she looked in the mirror and saw that her Afro rivaled the size and shape of her boyfriend Nate's. She walked out of the Y and into the Harlem streets where her Afro became just one of many and finally thought that she looked how she felt inside.

My mother arrived home to her mother with a self-satisfied look on her face, new loose curls encircling her head, and the money my grandmother gave her to pay Miss Lulene still in her purse. She had saved her own money to get the Afro. She took out the bills and approached my grandmother.

"Here, Ma. Thank you," she said, placing the dollars in her mother's hand. My grandmother took the money but said nothing; she simply stared at my mother's hair, dumbfounded and insulted, as if a strange man had walked up to her on the street and kissed her full on the lips. Suddenly realizing what had just happened, my grandmother stiffened the hand not holding the bills and slapped my mother clear across her face.

"Why did you do it?! Why did you do it?!" she screamed.

My mother, feeling the sting of the slap along with her mother's profound disappointment, cried. Tears snuck from my grandmother's eyes, too. To her, my mother's Afro was like getting a hundred runs in her favorite pantyhose, making a dozen trips downtown wearing dungarees, like my mother being caught a thousand times in the wrong outfit at school. My grandmother saw that the armor of propriety she'd tried to shield my mother's blackness with was completely off, making her vulnerable. She couldn't stand it.

"If you wanted an Afro, I would've bought you an Afro wig," she said with voice quaking.

The proposition seemed silly to my mother even then. Her world was becoming more volatile by the day. Following King and Kennedy's assassinations, there was a rash of violence involving and against the Black Panthers that left several young black people dead. During her sophomore year, four Kent State University students had been shot and killed during a protest. She, like many others, was reading *The Autobiography of Malcolm X*, and the impact of his life and his murder was a phenomenon she was still trying to comprehend. There was real danger and what appeared to be real revolution all around her. What would she have looked like with a fake Afro?

She thought her mother didn't understand—or didn't care to. "Joanna, you are to take yourself back to Miss Lulene's and have that thing washed out and your hair pressed and curled," my grandmother said. "No daughter of mine will walk around looking like a target."

My grandfather, who had been quietly standing by, suddenly piped up. "Oh, I think it looks nice," he said, with the gentle sway of the tobacco leaf fields he left in Douglas, Georgia, still evident in his southern lilt decades after he boarded a train to New York City for more opportunity and more freedoms.

"Yeah, it looks good," echoed her brothers.

But my grandmother's mind was made up. And she clearly was the one in charge: "Pressed and curled. Do you understand?"

Miss Lulene's was already closed by then, but the next day, my mother knew she would have to go.

"Yes, Mom," she answered.

And my mother felt her flirtation with teenage rebellion wilt under her mother's pressure, just as her Afro would the next day under the heat of Miss Lulene's straightening comb.

27

Better Muslim Than I

(

THE TELEPHONE RANG one Saturday or Sunday morning and, in the kitchen, Ummi picked it up.

"Hey, sis. Ramadan Karim!" she said, meaning it was one of the umtis, Haniya, Khadija, or Zainab. If Aliya had been around, she would've answered then handed Ummi the phone with defeat creeping into her voice. "It's Muslimhood," she would've said, hissing out the nickname she'd given our mother's Muslim cohort when we were younger. But Aliya had become an adult and was living on her own. Her knowledgeable disparagement of Islam now only came from a distance.

Ummi navigated the narrow runway of our kitchen, which had cabinets and a refrigerator on one side and more cabinets, a sink, a dishwasher, and a stove on the other, with the telephone nestled between her shoulder and her ear, as always.

"Naw, girl. Feeya's the only one fasting," she said, winking in my direction. "She's a better Muslim than I am." I figured then that she was speaking to Umti Khadija, the main member of Ummi's sisterhood who still, twenty-five years since becoming Muslim, adhered to Muslim practices—still wearing her khimar, still reading her Qur'an, still fasting for Ramadan. They all, however, held on to some aspects of their early days in the faith: their Muslim names, their Arabic lingo, their prayers to Allah, their belief in the Prophet, and, to a large extent, their unfettered love for each other.

I had just finished my breakfast, my suhoor, when Ummi spoke, and as the morning sky lightened from ocean blue to overcast gray, I remained seated at the dining room table. On the kitchen counter, Ummi whisked a bowl of batter she would later pour into circles that would bubble on a griddle and fill our apartment with the aroma of pancakes that she and Muhammad—but not I—would eat.

It was my first Ramadan. As a senior in high school at seventeen years old, I decided that if the rest of the Muslim world was fasting for Ramadan, then I would too. No one could deny me my Muslimness if I did what every other Muslim around the globe was supposed to do, I thought. And wasn't it about time? I was practically grown. Most Muslim kids start fasting when they reach puberty. I was long overdue. And for that matter, so were Ummi and Abi. They hadn't fasted since I didn't know when. I hoped that seeing me do it would inspire them to get back into the habit. If I succeeded and, at the same time, put myself on the straight path, I thought I'd surely gain favor with Allah. Doing the whole Ramadan thing seemed like a win-win.

Except that I only had a faint idea of what to do. It was clear that I couldn't eat or drink during daylight hours, but what exactly was considered daylight, I wondered? Was it when the sun first began its ascent, and the sky lightened from pitch black to midnight blue to ocean blue? Or was it when the sky had become visibly filled with bands of gold, yellow, and orange, and there was no more denying that day had broken? And what about sunset, when we were supposed to break the fast? Was it when the sun began its descent from high and swaths of red, orange, purple, and pink tinged the background of the clouds? Or was it when sunlight could no longer be seen amid the black of night?

For answers I couldn't figure out on my own, usually by scouring Ummi's shelves for some book or venturing around the corner to the library to find one there, I turned to my mother. She was always just down the hall or in another room nearby, but not always much help.

"Why didn't you wake me?" I whined to her one morning soon after Ramadan began, when I realized I had overslept. The sun was already unambiguously up, and I didn't have much time left to get ready for school.

"I didn't know you were fasting today."

Puzzled, I asked: "Well, why did you think I wasn't?"

"Because you were sleeping," my mother said, disregarding the catch-22 in her statement. It's true that I normally got up on my own, but when I didn't, she's the one who made sure I did. With a virtual shrug, Ummi went to the kitchen to continue preparing for work, and I rushed into the bathroom to brush my teeth. But then I stopped myself.

"Hey, Ummi," I called to her with my toothbrush in hand. "Does brushing your teeth break the fast?" I had missed my suhoor of oatmeal or Cream of Wheat, buttered toast, and sometimes turkey bacon while it was still dark outside, my only opportunity to eat before that evening's sunset. That was bad enough, but going outside without brushing my teeth? I cringed at the possibility of interacting for the entire day, through nine periods of high school, with funky breath. How would I talk to people? How could I smile?

"I don't know, Feeya," Ummi said from the kitchen.

"Well, what do you think? Should I brush my teeth?"

"Go ahead."

"But is that gonna break my fast?" I asked, distressed by her nonchalance.

"Well, let's see." Ummi approached and stood behind me in the bathroom doorway. "To make wudu, you have to wash out your mouth so I think you can do that. Yeah, wash out your mouth but don't use any toothpaste."

"Can I use my toothbrush?"

"I don't know," my mother said, frustrated.

I was losing patience with the lack of definitiveness in her answers, just as she was growing tired of my flurry of questions. So, naturally, I asked more: "Why don't you know? Haven't you done this before?"

"No, not really," she admitted. "At the time I would have been fasting, I was always pregnant or nursing one of you, so I haven't actually done Ramadan before. Maybe once." Ummi turned away breezily and continued to ready herself for work.

"Great," I said, realizing I was dealing with an amateur who didn't know much more than I did.

And then I understood: Ummi got so flustered every time I asked her questions about Islam not only because it might've been painful for her to remember—although I suspected that still had a lot to do with it—but because she didn't know the answers. I was putting her on the spot, and she didn't know how to respond. An image of my mother as a young woman came to mind, with a child at each of her hips, one filling her womb, and another—me—in her arms as the long, loose clothes and khimar I saw her wear in photographs draped over and threatened to cover both me and her. I wondered how many other Muslim women covered their questions, their doubts, their inexperience in layers of cotton, rayon, and polyester.

Accepting that I would be on my own in my pursuit of Islam, I turned on the faucet, dipped my toothbrush in the water, and ran it over my teeth, gums, and tongue. Almost immediately, my fast felt broken; there was enough toothpaste residue in the bristles for the slight minty taste to refresh me. I had gone too far, I thought, and Allah would not be pleased.

If I overslept again and Ummi would not help me investigate the faith I felt drawn to but she distanced herself from, I vowed to only use water and maybe a finger to prepare my mouth for the coming fast.

28

Making Waves

I SAT ON THE RED-CARPETED STEPS next to the ironwork railing in my father's house holding a fat white envelope in my hands. I need only feel the heft and textures of the stack of papers inside to understand what it meant. On top was a thick, striated, cream-colored page adorned with a navy blue-and-red seal telling me I had been accepted to Howard University. The letter was much the same as all the others I had received: "Congratulations. We are pleased to . . ." Behind it was a statement from financial aid, noting how much money the school would give me. Now this was something different.

"Tuition scholarship," it read.

"What kind of scholarship do you have?" I asked my brother, Isa, who had rescued the envelope from Abi's pile of neglected mail, urged me to open it, and now stood across from me as I did. He went to Howard—had just finished his sophomore year as a business school major there. The pinnacle of the black college bus tours he'd started, taking loads of high schoolers from New York down South to experience *A Different World* for a week firsthand, was always Howard. Maybe it was because he couldn't contain how much he loved the school, how much he felt he belonged there and nowhere else. I thought his right hand must've gotten sore with how many people he gave dap to on campus; his mouth must've gone dry with how much he boasted about the school's history, present, and future; his pull must've been stretched to the limit with all the perks he went out of his way to provide. I'd taken Isa's bus tour with my friends the previous fall; then, at his insistence, applied to Howard that winter. But I had no intention of going.

It wasn't that I didn't think Howard was a good school. I was just tired of following Isa. Every teacher who'd had him three years before they had me acted as if he had been the way, the truth, and the life. Automatically, without fail, they expected more from me than any other kid in class.

When calling roll the first day, they would look down at their roster, get a glimmer in their eyes upon seeing the first last name, look up with a smile on their face, and ask: "Oh, you're Isa's sister?" It became code for *"We expect brilliance, charm, and leadership from you. Anything less and this class—and your future in it—is doomed."*

I could not deliver. I was smart, but reserved, and much preferred to keep to myself than fill the classroom with bombast and clever ideas. Everything I did paled in comparison to my brother.

"Tuition and room and board," he answered. It had already begun.

"So this is not as good."

"But it's still good, Feeya. How much are those other schools offering you? A couple of thousand here and there?"

"Not tuition," I confirmed.

Isa left me sitting on the stairs to consider the choice I had on my own for a while. Whatever I decided, it would be my decision. I would spend the next four years, and then only the rest of my life, living with it.

I flipped through the other papers in the packet, curious to find any good reason to decline a full tuition scholarship that I knew would save my parents the burden of going into debt trying to provide me with a college education. I turned to the back of a glossy brochure that had printed in tiny black letters the name of every student organization on campus. I scoured it for groups that Isa wouldn't have joined, people who wouldn't know my brother before they knew me, places I could make my own impression and forge my own identity.

Because I'd decided I wanted to be a journalist, I only applied to schools with journalism—or at least good communications—programs. Howard had a newspaper: *The Hilltop.* I spotted its name in one of the long columns that began to support the notion that there could be a place for me at Howard. Isa had no interest in newspapers. From what

I understood, he'd carved out a place for himself at the School of Business, or "School of B" as he called it, and on campus, it was not near the School of Communications, or "School of C," where I'd spend most of my time. That was a good start. But I wanted more. I kept looking for how else I could escape Isa's long shadow at Howard. I continued searching the list of organization names darkening the back page of the brochure and stopped when I came across the word "Muslim."

"Muslim Students Association" read the full entry.

Oh, there's Muslims there? I thought, wondering why that idea hadn't occurred to me sooner. *And they must be black.*

"Hmm. Cool," I said to myself. I imagined a group of students—the women in khimars, the men in leather jackets—stalking the campus filled with activism and purpose, not unlike Ummi and Abi themselves and the cohort of friends they had made when they became Muslim, when they were my age some twenty-five years earlier. Suddenly, Howard became a bit more attractive.

Maybe I would join this group of students, I thought. Maybe they could help me claim the Muslim identity I felt belonged to me but that I had a hard time identifying as my own.

I recognized that for a while, I had only been dipping my toe in the pool of Islam. Maybe at college—away from the people I knew and their lack of encouragement, and separated from my reluctance to make waves—I would be brave enough to at least wade in the water.

29

Islamic Sensibility

ONCE MY MOTHER STARTED going to Banu-Hilal Herbal Tea Room, she got hooked on it. After classes at City College, she'd walk the four blocks down Convent Avenue, climb the ironwork staircase, order her treats, and find a seat illuminated by sunshine from the picture window. The place had an aura she liked, one that emphasized its Islamic sensibilities, just as she was beginning to herself. My mother felt at peace there, except that as she became a regular, her peace was regularly interrupted by what became a familiar mantra of several of the brothers who recognized her from MIB's jummah services.

"Sister," they'd start, "in Islam if you're seeing someone, it's supposed to be with the intentions of marriage." It seemed that everyone at Black Seeds Cultural Center, a community room in the basement of Harlem's St. Nicholas public housing project, where MIB now held its jummahs, knew about her relationship with Salahuddin. And none approved. "Are you intended?" they'd ask.

When my mother answered that she didn't have an intended husband, it seemed as if the brothers took that as their cue that she was looking for one. She deflected advances from all sorts: the mosque's Arabic teacher, members of its security department, members of its economics department, and the creator of the tearoom himself, my father, Hasan.

"You know, sister, there is no casual dating in Islam," he told her. My father was repeating what he said to every other attractive single sister who came around MIB after he'd decided to end a transitory marriage to the mother of his first son and start looking for a new wife. "If there were to be a date, it would have to be chaperoned," my father added, with hopes that the young lady with the warm smile and unique sense of style before him would take his bait and go on one of those chaperoned dates with him. He knew his chances were slim because my mother already had a boyfriend, and he wasn't the only brother who had his eye on stealing her from him.

My mother paid my father and all the other advancing brothers no mind. She was on to their rap and simply told herself, *You know what? I better stop going to that tearoom.*

She couldn't stay away, though. Even with the badgering and all the unwanted attention, there was something about Islam and the Mosque of Islamic Brotherhood that spoke to her. She felt it at the tearoom and during jummah services; when she walked with her City College friends, Betty and Latifa, wearing a khimar wrapped the way Latifa had shown her; and when she read the Qur'an with them. My mother read about Muslims' faith in one God and the Day of Judgment. And about their belief in the Prophet Muhammad and all the prophets who came before him, from Ibrahim (Abraham) to Isa (Jesus). Even though Jesus lost the divinity afforded him in the Bible, my mother was struck by how many of the Old Testament lessons she remembered from Sunday school were reflected in the Qur'an; she was struck by the inclusivity. She read about the pillar of hajj and imagined how unifying it must feel to have Muslims from all over the world convene in one Holy Land.

The more she read about and understood Islam, the more it resonated with her. She felt Muslim. Salahuddin's insistence that she become Muslim might have pushed her down the road a little faster than planned, but she recognized the path was leading her there anyway. No one had to tell her anything; she just felt it.

So, as Salahuddin and his friend Mikail had before her, she too made the decision to take shahada and officially become Muslim. It was December 1972, at the end of her first semester at City College and not long before her eighteenth birthday, when she shared her decision with her parents.

"Those types of religions are for misfits and oddballs, Jody," her mother said upon hearing the news. "I don't know why you want to do this."

She did it anyway.

30

What's in a Name?

$$\smile$$

ON THE FIRST DAY of Arabic class at Howard University, I took a seat in our classroom on the second floor of Douglass Hall wearing too-tight jeans, a T-shirt, and cowrie shell earrings, with my dark hair shaped up into a short Afro. My classmates, who chatted with each other as if they'd been acquainted long before coming to campus, entered sporting beards and thawbs, kufis and khimars. I smiled at them but said nothing until the professor, a schlubby-looking Middle Eastern man with a paunch and a cascade of oily jet-black hair, called roll.

"Abdur-Rahman," he said with an accent appropriate for an Arabic professor and, without noticing the curious glances and looks of mild shock that came over my classmates' faces until after the professor moved on to the next name, I answered with a crisp overenunciated, "Here."

Almost every other name I heard him call as he continued down the attendance sheet was distinctly American. Harris: "Here." Johnson: "Right here." And Washington: "Present."

But their first names were Shahid, Aminah, Aqil, Karima. Arabic. They were like the names I'd grown up pronouncing; ones that implanted themselves in my memory with less effort than all the Johns, Jameses, or Jens I'd met; ones that like the cozy nook in the corner of my mother's couch were so familiar to me they conjured comfortable images of home.

And that was why they all eyed me strangely when I was the one who answered to "Abdur-Rahman," I soon realized. With a name like that, they knew I had to be Muslim. But unlike them, I didn't look the part.

"OK, class. Today we learn the alphabet," the professor said, and I opened my spiral notebook to begin taking notes. But no sooner than he uttered "alif, ba, ta" did I lower my chin and chuckle into my chest, thinking back to my brief instruction from Abi, the Marvin Gaye of Arabic ABCs. I would be more serious this time, though, more mature, I reminded myself.

When I first saw Arabic I listed in Howard's course offerings booklet, I knew Allah was giving me an opportunity. He knew I still wanted to learn the language of the Qur'an and the vocabulary of Islam. Off at college, away from my family's religious indifference, I felt ready to let the cool waters of the pool of Islam lap up at least to my knees. Allah was giving me a second chance to do so. Without hesitation, I registered for the class.

Remembering this, I lifted my eyes to the chalkboard and earnestly began copying the curves and dots of each Arabic character.

Those first couple weeks, my Arabic class sped through the alphabet, introductory phrases, and commonly used words. Learning the characters that first day was the only time my classmates and I had been allowed to transliterate; for everything else, we were expected to remember the sound each character made and write only the Arabic and its English translation in our notes. It was hard, but I did it. And though I was doing well in class, I felt overwhelmed.

Following class one day, I stood by my desk on the side of the room where the female students usually gathered, stuffing books into my bag. My head was spinning with the day's information when Karima, one of my classmates, approached me. She was rather stocky, with a full figure, a medium brown complexion, and thick eyebrows; and she wore a brightly colored khimar wrapped tightly around her cherubic face. She was always outspoken during class, stopping the professor to ask more questions than anyone else.

"Where are you from?" Karima asked me.

"Long Island, New York," I said, having already learned since being on campus to differentiate my suburban upbringing from that of the students from one of the five boroughs. Their sensibilities were offended when I simply said I was from New York.

"Where did you get a name like Abdur-Rahman?" she said, with perfect inflections in all the right places. No stranger had ever pronounced it so well before.

"My parents converted when they were teenagers."

"Oh. So you're Muslim," she said matter-of-factly.

"Yeah," I said. "I was born Muslim," I added as explanation, sure that the difference between Karima and me, as Muslims, was as obvious to her as it was to me.

"You should come to jummah with us on Friday. It's right over here in the Carnegie Building," she said, pointing. "Everybody's really friendly."

I had no clue what building she was talking about and wasn't even aware there were jummah services on campus. I hadn't been at school that long, but so far, I wasn't as proactive about seeking out Islam as I had planned. Besides going to Arabic class and studying my lessons, I hadn't done anything to further my search. Stepping out of my comfort zone of inaction and passivity was harder than it seemed. Recognizing Allah at work to help break me of my habits, I was glad Karima approached me.

"OK," I smiled at her. "That sounds good."

31

The Stars Align

(

THE SPOT MY FATHER PICKED was well researched: the corner of East 149th Street and Third Avenue in the Bronx, a popular shopping hub. People walked by, traveling to and from stores, carrying shopping bags and lists, ready and often willing to spend money. This was where he set up his vendor's table one warm fall afternoon in 1972 and stocked it with wind-up trains. Kids loved to stop and watch him demonstrate how they worked. He was doing brisk business: winding up a train, watching a child's face burst into grinning as the locomotive chugged along the table, and then collecting the bills from parents who hoped the brief display of joy, becoming too rare a vision from their growing children, could be recreated in their own homes.

Even amid all this activity, my father had no trouble spotting the woman who walked in flowing fabric among the crowd of bell-bottoms and trench coats in his direction. *Hey, there's that sister that's involved with that guy,* he thought, remembering my mother from the mosque at Black Seeds.

"Hey, sister. How you doing?" he called to her.

My mother, who'd just gotten off the bus to do some shopping in the area, recognized the young man in the long cotton thawb and crocheted kufi, with sparse hairs on his cheeks and chin, as one of the badgering brothers from the tearoom.

"As-salaaumu'alaikum, brother. How are you?" she greeted him.

Without all the brothers he was usually surrounded by at the tearoom, my mother thought he didn't seem like such a bad guy. She walked on, and the new friendly feeling he gave off went with her.

The next time the two saw each other in the tearoom several months later, after she had taken shahada, he approached her without pretense.

"Hey, sister. Would you like to go out on a date with me?"

"Why, sure," my mother answered, refreshed by his directness.

They went, unchaperoned, for a vegetarian dinner at a Greenwich Village restaurant. As just the two of them sat together, far downtown from the tearoom and the mosque, miles apart from the brothers and sisters who knew them and the parents who raised them, they talked and tried to get to know each other.

"So, what made you start coming to the tearoom?" my father asked.

"Well, Salahuddin told me about it at first. Said they give some real good talks on Islam there. And it's just down the hill from my school— I go to City College. So I just started stopping in with a girlfriend of mine, real good sister, her name is Latifa. She introduced me to Islam, you know. What about you, Hasan? Why did you start going there?"

"I started it," he answered, and a smile, a mischievous smirk that betrayed the pride he felt about his creation, spread across his face.

"Huh? What do you mean?"

"It's mine. I started it. Well, it was mine before I gave it to the mosque, but the tearoom was my idea. Really Tawfiq's. We were driving in his car one day, and he mentioned this idea he had for a tearoom. I thought, *Hey, that's a good idea. I could do something with that.* And he didn't do anything about it, so I built it with my partner, Abdul-Malik. And when the mosque saw it was doing well and wanted to take over, we let them. For the good of MIB."

My father did not tell her that the money for the storefront's lease had come from his father. He did not tell my mother of his father's hope that owning his own business would give my father a way to provide for his budding family. He did not tell her of the furor that overtook my grandfather when he learned that my father had turned the business, which he'd named Banu-Hilal in solidarity with MIB businesses, over to the mosque when they requested it, without his asking for even a dime.

"Oh. Well, it's a nice place, a real nice place." My mother might have added how much she liked the pastries and how she was a baker herself. She could've talked about the clothes for sale at the tearoom and how she also enjoyed sewing.

"So what do you do now?" she asked.

My father explained that he'd recently begun an electrical apprenticeship. After first going into business with Abdul-Malik selling incense and essential oils in the East Village before they opened the tearoom, my father was finally heeding his father's advice to pursue a trade. Then, he could start a career that would allow him to provide for his family.

"I have two boys, you know. Idris is a year and a half and Aqil is just a baby. They live with their mother now, but one day, I'd like them to come and live with me, insha'Allah. Do you like kids, Joanna?"

"Oh, I love kids," my mother answered, undeterred by my father's already having a family, one that he was breaking up. "I'd like to have four. I have three brothers myself, and we're all pretty close. With our cousins, too. They're around the same age as us, and we all grew up like brothers and sisters."

"Really? I've always dreamed of having six," my father said, realizing that by adding my mother's wish to his own, their dreams were already aligned. "I have one brother, but he's so much younger than me that I basically grew up as an only child. So, when's your birthday?" my father asked. Astrology was one of his hobbies, and he wanted to see whether their stars aligned in any other way.

"December twenty-eighth," my mother answered; it had just passed.

"Nah, no it isn't," my father said.

"Yeah, December 28, 1954," she insisted.

"Nah, you're lying," my father said in disbelief.

"Why? When's yours?"

"December twenty-eighth. Nineteen-fifty."

The coincidence seemed so strange yet so perfect that they both thought for a moment that it had to have been arranged. But it couldn't have been. Unless by God. My mother then figured that encountering such coordination, such symmetry in two people who before that night had been strangers, must have been a sign from the Creator.

He could be the one, she thought. *This could be interesting.*

My mother tells me it was shortly after this date with my father that she broke up with Salahuddin. He was a nice guy, she said, but she felt he had no depth and no direction. She wanted a man with dreams. She was attracted to ambition, and my father, a couple of years earlier when he was just twenty, had opened a successful business—one she really liked.

My father tells me it was after his relationship with my mother got serious that he told her she had to make a decision between him and her boyfriend. And, in his words, "She dropped the other bum and said, 'OK. You're the guy. I got a real brother right here.'"

Either way, my mother wanted a big dreamer, and my father specialized in big dreams. My father, who'd been disappointed in what he saw as his first wife's lack of ambition and reluctance to fully embrace Islam, wanted a traditional wife; my mother reveled in sewing and cooking and in the idea of, one day, mothering. After a few months of seeing each other, they decided they were a good match.

My father, who'd gotten his first wife pregnant before marrying her, was eager to do things by the book this time. He traveled to my mother's apartment in the Bronx one day to talk to my grandparents about how he and my mother felt about each other and their future together.

"I love your daughter very much, and she and I would like to get married," he told them.

My grandmother glared at the young man sitting across from her: strange foreign clothing, unkempt facial hair, too old for her teenage daughter—her baby. And on top of all that, he'd already been married and divorced. He had two little boys of his own. Seeing all her dreams for my mother to be her college-educated, last-chance child evaporate and her fears for her as a teenage mom with nothing to fall back on materialize, my grandmother looked across the room at my mother with disappointment like a shadow on her face.

She asked, "Well, do you have to?" My grandmother wanted to know whether my mother was expecting. With the shape-concealing clothing my mother had gotten into the habit of wearing, my grandmother couldn't tell.

"No, Mom. I don't have to." The couple actually hadn't made their relationship physical yet.

"Then why do y'all feel you need to get married?" my grandmother asked.

My mother tried to explain that the courtship process so familiar to American teens and young adults, one she and her ex-boyfriends had gladly participated in, didn't exist in Islam.

"If you're seeing somebody, it's with the intention of marriage," she said, hearing herself echo what the brothers in the tearoom had told her so often only after she'd already said it.

My grandmother still didn't understand what the big rush was for. Remembering the rumors about ex-con Black Muslims and revolutionaries changing their names to escape criminal pasts, she was suspicious and had been ever since she found out about my mother's dating this Muslim. Now with him before her, my grandmother decided to conduct an interrogation.

"What is your real name?" she asked, and my mother cringed with embarrassment.

"The name I was born with is Robert Nesbitt Jr. But my real name now, the name I took when I became Muslim, is Hasan Idris Abdur-Rahman." My father would add another s to become Hassan later, to differentiate himself from the several Hasans in the mosque and to force correct pronunciation, with the stress on the second syllable, not the first. Claiming this new identity would not be a matter of court petitions or legal forms; he simply owned it, speaking it into existence and writing it as if it had always been his.

"Where are you from?" my grandmother continued, unsatisfied.

"I'm from here. I was born in Harlem but grew up mostly in the Bronx. Not too far from here."

"Who are your parents? Do I know them?"

For each of my grandmother's questions, my father had a patient, thorough answer that put, at least, my mother's mind at ease. The man she wanted to marry could stand up for himself.

My grandfather, who'd been sitting quietly while he took everything in, turned to my mother, his only daughter, daddy's little girl. He asked her only one question: "Well, do you feel ready to be a responsible wife and mother?"

"Yes, Dad. I do."

32

Meant to Be

ON A WARM FRIDAY AFTERNOON, I walked up the wide stone staircase of the Carnegie Building, a relatively small brick hall with a couple of stone columns out front at the edge of the "Yard" on the main campus. I opened the brown-tinted glass door and, just inside, nearly stumbled on a jumble of abandoned shoes in all sizes, styles, and conditions: worn loafers, low-budget sneakers, sensible heels. I was supposed to remove mine too, I guessed, nervous that at my first jummah here, I would commit some faux pas that would bar me from ever showing my face again. Hesitantly, I kicked off my footwear and added them to the pile.

I stepped lightly in stockinged feet beyond the tiny vestibule into a simple, unfurnished, carpeted room, similar to the mosque barren of furniture I had once visited in Long Island with my family when I was little. Long windows on adjacent walls both faced away from the sun, tinting the room a dim orange despite the bright sunny day.

I had never seen a soul enter or exit the building before that day and figured nobody on campus actually used it. But like a meeting of a secret society, all the black Muslim students I had noticed on my way to or from class in the previous weeks were present inside. So were a handful of older blacks I didn't recognize who might have been faculty, staff, or graduate students, and some who looked Middle Eastern, Indian, Pakistani, and North African. Howard had the nickname "the Mecca," and seeing the mosaic of Muslims who'd flocked to the masjid that day for jummah, I imagined there was another reason besides the school's reputation as the epicenter of black education.

Conscious of my button-down shirt, long skirt, and multicolored African print headwrap with a bun at the back—my attempt at dressing appropriately for the mosque—I pushed past the noisy clusters of men congregated at the front of the room. Not wanting to appear lost, I quickly took a seat on the floor beside a couple of friendly looking middle-aged ladies quietly stationed in the back.

This separation of the sexes also brought me back to the mosque I visited when I was young, the only time before this day I remembered being inside one. Except that there, when it was time to pray, a sudden buzz cut through the murmurs like tires whirring in the rain as someone drew a thin sheetlike curtain diagonally across the room, partitioning the women from the men. My mother, sister, and I clung close on one side, while my father and brothers got pushed to the other. Through the shroud, I could make out the silhouettes of men and boys, but I could no longer tell stranger from family.

When would Karima get there? I worried, smiling awkwardly at the olive-skinned women to my left, wondering if they would be my guides if my classmate didn't show up. But then Karima came, just as she said she would, and sat down next to me. I had no reason to doubt her.

"*Allahu akbar.*" The call to prayer rang out and quickly grabbed everyone's attention. "*Allahu akbar.*" The dips and waves in the muezzin's voice were like a thumb and forefinger gently clamped to the top of my ear that politely, but forcefully, compelled me to listen. "*Ashadu'an la illaha illa Allah . . .*" And then the meaning of the words he sang registered: God is great. God is great. I bear witness that there is no god but Allah . . . "*Ashadu'ana Muhammadan rasul Allah . . .*" I bear witness that Muhammad is the messenger of Allah . . .

I was not in the habit of listening to the adhan, but somehow it was as familiar to me as my brother's balls-of-his-feet bouncy walk that I could spot from across the Yard without really looking. Even in a crowd and among distractions, that strut and this call were unmistakable.

The call went on, and with much commotion everybody began filing downstairs into the men's and ladies' rooms. We would have to make wudu before we prayed; my mother had mentioned the cleansing ritual to me over the phone when I told her, nonchalantly, that I would be coming to jummah.

"Oh, that's beautiful," she'd said in one breath. And then, "You sure you want to do that, Feeya?" she asked in another, probably realizing that whatever I experienced, she would not be able to protect me from or guide my understanding of it.

"Yeah, why not?" I brushed her off, confident that her absence was exactly what I wanted.

I didn't understand what the big rush downstairs was for until I saw the bathroom. It was tiny and clearly not made for such high capacity. Its wooden door opened right into the sinks, causing the person coming in to have to apologize for nearly knocking out whoever was standing behind it.

Nervous, I felt the sudden need to relieve myself and squeezed into one of the two narrow stalls. It locked with a brown cigarette-shaped sliding latch, as if the flat chrome locks common to public bathrooms everywhere by 1997 hadn't yet been invented. The thick, yellowed toilet seat appeared to have been there since decades before too. There were nice touches, though, like the miniature bouquet of fake flowers atop the toilet tank and the tiny watering can already filled with water. I took it all in with a deep breath, preparing to be exposed as an amateur Muslim as soon as I flushed and opened the stall door.

When I did, I was confronted with too many women crowding each other around the lonely duo of sinks, both with water running furiously from the faucets. I nudged and excused myself up to one of them, thinking that as I washed my hands, I could get the gist of how to make wudu. Discreetly, I watched the women beside me splash themselves with water while murmuring in Arabic, but I couldn't tell what they were saying or which body parts needed splashing or in what order or for how long.

"What am I supposed to do?" I finally decided to ask Karima, who was waiting her turn along with every other woman in the masjid.

"I thought you said you were raised Muslim. Didn't your parents teach you this?"

"I was born Muslim," I clarified, "but they didn't really teach me anything." It was embarrassing to admit, but I thought it better to just tell the truth than to pridefully pretend I knew things that I clearly didn't. I was there to learn.

With no other commentary, Karima gave me explicit instructions. I did what she said, saying "Bismillah," then washing my hands, my mouth, my nostrils, my face, and each arm up to the elbow, first right, then left, all three times. Next, I wiped a wet hand over my head once and around my ears. Last, I washed each foot three times, through my perfectly hued pantyhose, again right first, then left. Although I'd read about making wudu before prayer in *The Muslim Primer*, my parents had never shown me how to do it. Grabbing a paper towel to dry myself off, I had to question why they hadn't.

Karima and I and the rest of the ladies, purified for prayer, filtered back upstairs, where I readied myself for the next wave of embarrassment. There seemed to be so much I didn't know about Islam but should have. We women arranged ourselves shoulder to shoulder in slanted lines at the rear of the empty room. The men stood in similar rows before us, only their backs and the backs of their heads visible from my vantage point. Each row was slightly off kilter because we were all facing east, toward Mecca, to make salat.

The prayer began simply enough. We all raised our hands to our ears and said, "Allahu akbar." After doing that once more, we folded our arms over our torsos and finally did something for which I needed no guidance: reciting al-Fatihah, the prayer I had learned as a kid. As I grew up, I held on to this act that had always brought me solace, like a baby latched to its mother's breast, for nourishment, yes, but also comfort. While I still prayed by myself occasionally, I hadn't prayed with anyone else in years. And I had never prayed with so many people before.

"*Iyyaka na-buduwa, iyyaka nasta'iyn.*" I pushed out the sentence I had once forgotten and from every corner of the room, it echoed back to me.

The isolation of female voices coming from where I was standing, combined with the deep male tones reflecting off of the front wall, reminded me of rehearsals from my junior high school chorus. There was power in our combined breath. This must be why Muslims in every area of the world pray at the same five times each day, I thought; unified and continual, their prayers must ring in Allah's ears, an inescapable beseeching worthy of His attention.

After the last words of Surat al-Fatihah, everybody raised their hands to their ears again. "Allahu akbar," they said, then bent over at the waist, placing their hands on their knees. I followed along. But with the split-second delay in my movements, I felt it was obvious to all the women standing beside and behind me that I didn't know what I was doing.

Next, we all straightened ourselves. "Allahu akbar," we said with our hands at our ears. Then we knelt all the way down to the floor, touching our foreheads before us on the ground. "Allahu akbar," we said, ending the prayer.

Everyone lifted their upper bodies to an upright position, where I thought we would finally hold our silent prayers. But before I knew what was going on, everyone pressed their heads back to the floor. I nearly gave myself a concussion throwing my forehead down, trying to catch up. "Allahu akbar," we said for a final time.

The remaining segments of the prayer again transported me to my family's living room in Baldwin. From my spot on the sheet-covered couch, I remembered parting my eyes as our prayer drew to a close and seeing Ummi crouched on the floor with eyes shut and both palms on her lap. Her right index finger was raised and wiggling, as though dancing to a soundless tune. She was silent and appeared to be entranced. But when I asked her later what she'd been doing, she told me the words of her muted prayer.

"La illaha illa Allah. Muhammadan rasul Allah." I repeated the chant my mother had taught me to quietly focus my mind on while I rotated my pointer finger on my lap. The sisters around me did the same until the time for silent prayers was over.

Ummi did not get up then. I kept watching her as she and Abi twisted their heads from one side of their bodies to the other, as if pulled by an invisible force. On each side, they said something into the air: "As-salaamu'alaikum wa rahmatullah." Each row of worshippers turned our chins to our right shoulders, as if greeting the neighbor on our right. Then, still seated with legs tucked beneath us, we shifted our chins to the left shoulders and symbolically offered that neighbor the same: "May the peace and mercy of Allah be unto you."

Adjusting ourselves out of prayer positions but remaining in our spots on the floor, everyone listened as the imam, who had gray in his beard and under his kufi and was dressed in a West African-style buba, gave his khutbah. I have no recollection of it. My mind was elsewhere.

Even after jummah ended and I gave my salaams to Karima, collected my shoes, and walked along the pebbly paths from the Carnegie Building down the hill to my dorm room in the Quad, my mind was elsewhere. It was on the water I didn't know where to splash while making wudu; it was on the prostrations I didn't know how to make during salat; it was on the Arabic I didn't know how to say and didn't try to utter during the prayer. What kind of Muslim could I possibly be, I asked myself, when there was so much I didn't know about Islam?

The farther away I walked, the more upset I became. I was mad at myself for not knowing, but I was also mad at Ummi and Abi. Making my way up to my dorm room on the second floor of Frazier Hall, I had to wonder why I'd grown up without knowledge of some of the most basic practices of Islam. I just didn't understand why they had left so much out of what they taught me about being Muslim.

Did my parents intend for me to discover this stuff on my own, as they did when they converted when they were around eighteen, my age then? Or was there just too much to teach to even begin the process with Aliya, Isa, Muhammad, and me? Or did they never want us to explore the rituals of Islam, having abandoned them themselves so many years before? I unlocked my door, untied my headwrap, and plopped myself on my bed, overburdened with questions. Staring up at the ceiling, I had no answers, only the distinct feeling that my parents had left me ignorant of a big part of who I was, or at least who I felt I was meant to be.

33

No Turning Back

MY MOTHER WAS BEGINNING to understand what she'd gotten herself into.

"Hasan wants me to make his suit for the wedding," she told her friend Latifa when they got together to shop for the fabric she'd use to make her wedding dress.

"What? He does?" Latifa, three years older than my mother, had already been married for a few years by then.

"Yeah, girl. He asked for brown, with a Nehru collar, and trim along the lapel and down the pant legs."

"Oooh, are you gonna do it?"

"Yeah," my mother answered. "He already asked me if I would do his laundry for him, you know."

"What? He didn't."

"Yes, he did. He said, 'Nowadays, you can hardly find women who want to do that stuff,'" she said, mimicking my father's dull tone. She and Latifa laughed, but my mother had indeed washed her fiancé's dirty clothes—for the first time of many, she figured. And now she was searching through bolts and spools of brown, from tan to dark chocolate, trying to find the right shade and texture for his suit.

As she and Latifa scoured the Indian store, each on a mission to find the right cloth, perhaps Latifa stopped and tilted down a bolt of pink cotton from the tight row of solids before her. "You like this one, Jody?" she would have asked.

My mother went closer and rubbed the material between her thumb and forefinger. The gold and diamond engagement ring that my grandfather had once given my grandmother and that my father, in proposing, had given her shone from her ring finger.

"I hope you don't mind sleeping on the floor," my grandmother had told my mother in her gruff tone when they first met. "'Cause Robbie likes to sleep on the floor."

My mother pushed the bolt back in line with the others. Though only eighteen, she was experienced in picking cloth and knew what she wanted. "It's a little too heavy, don't you think? I'm looking for something lighter. Like a bride," she might have said as she faced the narrow aisles to find the chiffons, charmeuses, and taffetas. She discovered them out of view of the entrance, away from all the dust, grime, and foot traffic that could have soiled them. She eyed the whites, side by side with off-whites, creams, ivories, and even beiges, but none satisfied her. She had something different in mind.

—————

When the wedding day arrived, Latifa showed up at my grandparents' apartment early. She'd been there several times before, always welcomed warmly by my grandparents' accustomed hospitality. This time, although neither knew whether there was such a thing in Islam, she was there to serve as my mother's maid-of-honor.

"The bodice looks good, Jody," Latifa said, as they stood in my mother's bedroom, facing the mirror from which the image of the soon-to-be-bride in the form-fitting pink jumper she made reflected back at them. Not long before, Latifa had visited United Nations headquarters in Manhattan and picked up a pamphlet on sari draping to prepare for the occasion. "How do you want me to wrap this?" she asked, holding out the pale pink chiffon my mother had settled on and added gold lamé trim to.

"Tight."

—————

The YWCA on 125th Street didn't look like much from the outside, only a simple storefront window amid a line of other simple storefront windows. But inside, two hundred Muslims—Taylors, Butlers, Nesbitts, and more—filled the space to witness two become one. More than anything, they were there to see the transformation of girl to woman, Joanna to Labiba, daughter to wife.

After the guests settled, my mother and father knelt before the officiate, as is Muslim custom. My father, donning an embroidered kufi and the sleek suit his fiancée had tailored in fabric the color of well-steeped black tea, bowed his head. My mother, on his right and wrapped in a chiffon sari-khimar combination the color of strawberry frosting, couldn't stop smiling.

My mother's mother sat somewhere across the room, trying to conceal that she was an erupting volcano. The first rumbles that had shaken her from her dormant state were my mother's changes of hair and wardrobe; the news that she was converting to Islam had produced tremors and a release of steam; my father's introduction and proposal caused her cool hard demeanor, sturdy as rock, to melt away; and now a wedding, at age eighteen, so close to her brothers', Kenny and Wade, weddings—which meant my grandmother couldn't possibly trouble her coworkers for gifts again—and not in a white wedding gown but a pink sari, sent sputters of burning hot lava out her top. My mother had recognized my grandmother's volatility but figured her wedding was her day. She refused to compromise.

It was time to exchange rings. In his hand, my father gripped a gold band for my mother embossed with the opening of al-Fatihah in Arabic: "In the name of Allah, the Beneficent, the Merciful." When spoken at the start of anything new, Muslims considered the words both a prayer and a blessing. My father, married, divorced, and already a father of two at age twenty-two, was eager for his second marriage to work; he needed both prayer and blessing. He slid the wide band on my mother's slender finger.

The officiate then placed a Mosque of Islamic Brotherhood marriage certificate before them. It stated that Hasan Idris Abdur-Rahman entered into a contract of marriage with Labiba Abdul-Ghafur—the Muslim name my mother had received just the day before, which, on that May day, 1973, became and would remain Labiba Abdur-Rahman.

"Qabul. Qabul," they both said, repeating their unequivocal acceptance of the contract. "Qabul."

Both their fathers, who were meeting for the first time at the ceremony, signed it, as did Imam Tawfiq and a couple other witnesses. Gazing at the completed certificate and realizing it meant she was now a married Muslim woman, my mother clutched her hand to her chest and beamed in astonishment. She had really done it this time. She had become the person she felt she was inside. And there would be no frantic visit to Miss Lulene's ever again, no easy way to set straight what might have gone awry. This time, there would be no turning back.

34

Dumb

(

IT WAS THE NIGHT BEFORE Martin Luther King Day, when all of DC's college students would be out of class and all of Washington's federal employees would be off from work—a perfect time to party. Leading up to it all week, clubs had promoted events for the night as if it would be the second coming of Howard's legendary homecoming weekend. Radio stations had advertised admission specials for days. Party promoters had blanketed the campus with fliers. Conversations around the dorms and in the caf eventually landed on plans for Sunday night. And when my friends and I saw the fancy chartered bus with tinted windows and plush seats idling outside our dorm, waiting to transport us freshman girls in style to the club that night, we knew we'd made the right decision not to miss out.

There were a lot of us. Usually, almost half the girls who lived on the second floor of Frazier Hall, my floor, and a handful of the ones who lived above us went out together. These girls, who had quickly become my closest friends, were a lot like my friends from home, loud and bold New Yorkers who liked to have fun and be the center of attention. I, naturally, was the quiet one. We called ourselves "Second-Floor Frazier" after our new home and did as much together as possible. That night, we packed into the bus, sang along loudly with the hip-hop pumping from the sound system, and as we arrived, peered out the windows to see a gaggle of men stalking the entrance as if anticipating a sighting of Tupac or Biggie.

They were waiting to get in, but also for us to show up—because what's a party without the presence of pretty girls? Upon our arrival, the men quickly turned our deboarding process into a show: We were the entertainment; they, the audience. They ogled row upon row of scantily clad college girls streaming from the bus and past them as though judging a beauty contest.

When it was my turn to step down, I knew I wouldn't get the kind of reception from the lusty crowd that my best friend, Sonya, would. She had a smile full of straight teeth, a face with sharp features, a small waist that separated her thick bottom from her stacked top, and walked with a high-heeled strut that let everyone see she knew she was bad.

"Uh! Woo!" the onlookers grunted and screwed up their faces, as if in a recording studio hearing a nasty beat for the first time, when she appeared in the bus's doorway and effortlessly negotiated her long legs down the steps.

I, on the other hand, was short and skinny, with a face that appeared even younger than my eighteen years and a grin full of gaps I was only self-conscious about at moments like this. I descended from the bus's entrance in my chunky platforms steadily, anxious to get my assessment over with.

"OK. OK," the guys offered polite encouragement and even a helpful handclap when they saw me, as if I'd just finished a mistake-riddled balance beam routine but at least managed not to fall off. I hustled through the frigid winter air following Sonya inside, thankful that at least no one laughed at or booed me as they did other girls.

Inside, the club was packed, and the thick, moist air rising from the hundreds of pulsating bodies put all thought of the cold outside to rest. It was dim, with just enough illumination trickling down from white-and-blue stage lights to tell whether the person dancing behind you had an attractive silhouette; it was not quite bright enough to see whether that person was actually attractive. The music played too loud for conversations, so instead, an exchange of single sentences had to be shouted directly into ears. The bass in the songs thumped through chests.

My friends and I scanned the dance floor for a good spot. Normally, that meant smack in the middle, center stage, as in a theater-in-the-round, where everyone passing through or radiating out from that point could watch us, the stars of the show. But it was too crowded for us to even make our way there this night. We split up, with a few of us moving into a room with a smaller dance floor and a lot fewer people. Sonya and I planted ourselves comfortably in the middle of it and started moving.

We were a good pair because we were opposites and usually attracted guys who were interested in either her or me, but not both. I was short, while she was tall; I was flat, while she was round; my hair was kinky and cropped, while hers was straight and long; I danced in an energetic hip-hop style, while her movements were decidedly alluring and graceful. But we were both A students from suburban areas of New York who loved hip-hop and to dance.

Mobb Deep's "Shook Ones Pt. II" came on, and I was transported back to New York, where the duo's songs were my I-may-be-little-but-I-can-be-tough theme music. As we bounced to the beat, two guys approached us: a tall one for her and a short one for me. They were clearly friends, as we were, and were mirroring our movements step for step. I glanced over at Sonya, flashing her a look of approval.

Week after week, I had become used to the disappointment of some stranger grabbing me on the dance floor and grinding his body against mine with no regard for the rhythm of the music or courtesy for personal space. I went to the club because I liked dancehall, loved hip-hop, and felt the urge to move whenever I heard them; for the first time in a long time, I had a partner who helped me showcase it. I was impressed. The club-goers surrounding us seemed to be moving in a wave, except instead of standing and raising both arms on cue, one after the other, they bounced from side-to-side in a basic two-step. Noticing the dance anomaly beside them, they began to back away and cleared a circle around Sonya, me, and our dance partners—enough room for us to really show what we could do. I felt as if I were in *House Party*.

With pressure on to deliver, I chose to ignore it by rapping hard with Havoc and Prodigy and doing all the moves I would've done in front of my bedroom mirror.

"*Son they shook. 'Cause ain't no such things as halfway crooks.*" I bobbed my head and bounced my shoulders and pointed my arms.

"*Scared to death or scared to look. They shook.*" I weaved my legs in and out, rocked my waist side-to-side, and bent my knees down to the floor.

My partner did all the same. He was good. I smiled. The crowd, standing at a distance, stared. We danced on. Our moves got more sophisticated, with him moving beside me, then behind me, but maintaining synchronicity. And then, like a record player needle dragging across vinyl and screeching all action to a halt, my big brother walked into the room.

My face must have dropped and my eyes gone wide, wondering what he was doing there. Isa never came to the club. He couldn't have come to get me, I thought—I hoped—and kept dancing. He hadn't seen me yet.

"Hey, isn't that your brother?" Sonya leaned over and spoke clearly into my ear.

There was no reason to answer. We both knew it was. Of all my siblings, Isa and I look the most alike. With one eye on my dance partner and the other on him, I watched my brother step through the crowd giving dap and pounds along his way because, of course, people there knew him. People everywhere knew him.

He was wearing his coat and scarf; he probably didn't plan on staying long, I figured. Then, frantic, I thought about what he would see me wearing: a pair of black spandex pants I'd gotten as part of the uniform for my high school step team and a favorite long-sleeve cotton shirt with a zipper at the neck. The long-sleeve shirt was a little more dressed than I normally was at the club. *Good*, I thought. I was practically a nun compared to the girls around me. *He can't get on me about that.*

Not even five feet away, Isa finally spotted me. He stopped walking and took a moment to stare me down. His face showed no surprise and no anger, just plain and simple disapproval.

But I didn't flinch. He wasn't going to mess up my good time this time, I thought, and danced harder than I had before. I rapped more, bounced harder, rocked deeper. My partner grabbed my waist, and we curved our hips toward each other, beat after beat.

Isa shook his head, then silently kept moving through the crowd.

I grinned. My big brother had caught me making a spectacle of myself in the middle of a club and he didn't say a word and he didn't do anything to stop it. I had won. I felt as if I'd finally shaken my role of "Isa's little sister" and become my own person. I knew I'd hear about our encounter later, but right then, that night, I was victorious. The song changed and the crowd closed in, ending my solo.

"I thought you were fasting for Ramadan," Isa said. After he'd seen me at the club, he called me up and invited me over to his apartment. Despite his living literally blocks away from me, just beyond the edge of campus, we rarely got together.

"I am," I said, sitting on Isa's couch, while he sat across from me in his desk chair. He must've heard I was fasting from Ummi or Abi, I figured, because I didn't tell him. "But that's during the day."

"So at night you go out and shake your ass in the club?" he said, more as statement than question, more as an accusation than an attempt to understand.

"If I feel like it." Because I had to be up at four in the morning anyway to eat suhoor and make the fajr prayer before each day of fasting began, it made perfect sense to me to stay awake till then and rest after the sun came up. Sure, it was unconventional, but I didn't see the problem.

"Feeya, you can't just be a Muslim when you feel like it. You have to take this seriously."

And there he was, the Isa I thought had shown up at the club had finally arrived to reprimand me and show me the error of my ways. But Isa wasn't a practicing Muslim. None of my siblings were. I was the only one who was even trying. Who was he to tell me that the way I was trying was wrong?

After that first time, when I fumbled my way through jummah on campus, I threw on a headwrap and went back for services in the Carnegie Building the following Friday and the next one and every one I could as long as I wasn't menstruating and was not supposed to pray inside the masjid. After missing out on so many jummahs growing up— so much lost practice and so much unacquired knowledge—I needed to catch up. I did, and in the process of learning how to pray and make wudu and understand surahs from the Qur'an, I made a couple more

Muslim friends. I'd looked forward to fasting with them for Ramadan when it began in December that year.

But by the time it started, school was on winter break; I was back home in New York fasting by myself again. When I returned to school in January, I kept up the fasting with my new Muslim friends, broke the fast at iftar with them each night, and went to jummah with them on Fridays. Then, on Saturday nights, I went clubbing with my dormitory friends. I probably should've seen a conflict between my religious interests and my secular ones, but I didn't.

Islam was always finding its way into hip-hop. Groups like Brand Nubian, A Tribe Called Quest, and the Fugees, and artists like Rakim, Queen Latifah, and Nas, through their names, styles, principles, and lyrical content, represented a New York / New Jersey, black Muslim aesthetic with which I identified. Listening to their references since I was a kid had added to my respect for and interest in the faith. Growing up, even our mother, who understood almost nothing hip-hop, got excited when she heard a rapper slip some Arabic into a song on the radio. I didn't see any problem.

"I am taking it seriously," I told Isa, still unable to grasp what exactly I'd done wrong. Already I knew that I wasn't a conventional Muslim—I didn't do anything conventionally—but I didn't feel I was actually breaking any rules. Except for my head, I'd made sure I was completely covered in the club; I didn't drink, didn't smoke; I wasn't having sex. "I was just dancing," I told Isa. After keeping our distance from each other at college, I could hardly stand the return to his overbearing big brother ways, trying to tell me what to do.

"Yeah but, Feeya. Think about it, did you see any other Muslims in the club just dancing?"

I took a moment to stop defending myself and actually think about what Isa was saying. *Were there any Muslims in the club?* I asked myself. *Would there be any Muslims in the club?* If they were traditional practitioners of the faith, I guessed there wouldn't be, because just as at jummah, men and women are to remain separate. If they are not related, they are not to hug, shake hands, or touch in any way.

Growing up where every male Muslim I knew was either my father, my brother, or like a brother, this distance wasn't something I'd thought about often. But Isa did. Rather, he thought about what he felt I should have been thinking about. Even as I tried to separate myself from him, he still remembered the lesson that Abi had spanked into us as children: He was my keeper.

"Do you? Do you see any other Muslims in the club dancing with you?" he asked.

The dancing, I would later learn, was also forbidden. I read that Muslims, female or male, are not supposed to dance in public. My heart fell to the pit of my stomach as I looked at the page and had to read the words again: "*Muslims are not to dance in public.*"

But I recalled that in third grade, I jerked my body to "Walk Like an Egyptian" in a way I thought white people could appreciate and, at a white friend's birthday party, still won the dance competition. In fourth grade, my friends and I spent hours choreographing a routine to Janet Jackson's "Control" for the school talent show and executed it to wild applause. In fifth grade, I started dressing up in leotards and tights for ballet, patent leather tap shoes for tap, and lappas and headwraps for African dance classes I loved. Throughout high school, the latest dancehall hit or hip-hop anthem from New York's golden era was sure to bring me, the quiet girl, off the wall at basement parties, sweet sixteens, or teen nights at clubs, enlivened by my connection to the music and indifferent to what anyone thought of me. But, no, I hadn't seen any Muslims dancing with me.

Isa knew that. And he knew that music and dance were some of my greatest joys. Yet he was trying to tell me I would have to give them up if I was to submit to Allah's will.

Maybe the whole Muslim thing was too much for me, I began to think. If being a Muslim meant I couldn't be who I was and couldn't do harmless things I liked to do, then maybe I wasn't meant to be a Muslim. After a few months of clarity, I went back to being as confused as ever.

I knew he wasn't trying to, but my brilliant brother still had a knack for making me feel stupid. That night, I left his place feeling dumber than ever.

35

The Spirit of Allah

☾

THE MORNING SKY was still dim with the remnants of night, the air cold enough to freeze the usual ebb and flow of campus. No one was outside; a single car here and there sputtered along the street, trailed by a plume of white smoke that dissipated with distance. Alternating red, yellow, and green glows from the traffic light that gently swayed with the wind were the only other sign that life, at a later time, on a warmer day, existed.

Yet I was up and out, shivering through my sheer-lined skirt and nude stockings while I waited for the shuttle bus to take me to Karima's dorm on the other side of campus. I reminded myself that I must've endured lower temperatures wearing fewer clothes while I stood in line to get into DC's best clubs with no jacket, trying, alongside my friends, to avoid the annoyance of a coat-check fee. Certainly, I could withstand the cold for this more righteous purpose. My grumbling stomach made it harder, though. I'd skipped breakfast to make sure I got to the bus stop on time. But with Ramadan finally over and heading to my first Eid al-Fitr celebration, I anticipated being able to eat soon, while the sun was up.

The shuttle sidled up to the curb, and climbing its ministairs and dropping onto its stiff seat in solitary silence, I couldn't help but think about the party bus that navigated my friends and me through the streets of DC while we sang songs and cracked jokes in plush-and-tinted style just weeks earlier. That was the last time I had been to the club. After my conversation with Isa, I decided it best to stay dorm-bound on club nights, at least for the rest of Ramadan.

The bus arrived at Karima's unfamiliar dorm. I went inside and found her room number in the eerie quiet of an upper floor. Softly, so as not to disturb any of her neighbors who might be asleep, I knocked on her door.

When it opened, she stood before me unfashionably cloaked, clearly a hasty effort to hide herself from potential male company. But once she saw that it was just me, she let me in, closed the door, and quickly dropped her impromptu head covering.

Karima dyes her hair? I thought, upon discovering what was beneath her khimar. It was rust brown, permed, nearly to her shoulders, and looked like it had been wrapped overnight. Our friend, Zakiyah, who was also in the room that morning, wasn't wearing her khimar yet either. Her dark hair zig-zagged in intricate, stylish cornrows. Outside that room no one would see their hair, I noted. Yet like other black women, they took pride in having a well-maintained and up-to-date coif. It surprised me; then I wondered why it did, because it wasn't like I didn't put on my best bra and panties that morning though I knew nobody but me would see them beneath my clothes.

"Did you have suhoor yet?" Karima asked me.

"No," I answered, and my hopes of eating during the daytime crashed to the bottom of my empty stomach. "I wasn't sure if we were fasting today."

"Well, you better hurry up. The sun is about to rise."

I grabbed a couple of slices of bread from the wheat loaf Karima had on her kitchen counter (these dorm rooms, so far from the amenities of campus, were equipped like studio apartments) and scarfed them down as fast as I could.

Karima picked up her iron and pressed it with a hiss onto her clothes, already carefully draped across the ironing board. We all had to look special that day. Karima, Zakiyah, and I were traveling with a group of Howard Muslims to the DC metropolitan area Eid gathering in Northern Virginia. It was supposed to be huge.

Among the hundreds of Muslims who'd be there, I anticipated gleaning a collective sense of completion I hadn't been able to achieve when I finished Ramadan on my own, as I did back home. Everybody there—blacks, Middle Easterners, whites—would have shared in the month-long sacrifice, and everybody—women, men, teens—would be equally relieved to see it end. We would congratulate each other. We would prostrate ourselves and thank Allah for giving us the strength to complete it. We—and here's what I looked forward to most—would be a "we" with a communal spirit of purpose and a unified feeling of accomplishment. And so, I was eager to go.

Karima and Zakiyah had stopped by my dorm room the day before to check my closet for something appropriate to wear. They knew I only covered when I went to jummah—out of respect, a sense of propriety, and because I wouldn't be let in otherwise—so my wardrobe of Muslim attire was limited. After marveling at all the inappropriate things I had—"Where do you wear this?" Karima asked pulling out an above-knee skirt—they picked out an ankle-length navy blue skirt adorned with cream-colored flowers that belled out at the bottom and a cream-colored button-down blouse that cinched at the waist. Realizing that I had no solid-colored khimars to match with such a formal outfit, only colorful African print fabrics to offset the usual basic solid clothes I preferred, Zakiyah offered to let me borrow one of hers. I was grateful.

As we three proceeded to get dressed up, Karima pressed play on her stereo.

"There are times when I look above and beyond, there are times when I feel your love around me, baby," Janet Jackson's voice seethed from the speakers. I recognized *The Velvet Rope* immediately; the same CD was in regular rotation in my stereo. Out of habit, and because I can't stand still when I hear a good beat, I began to bounce to the music.

"You dance like that to that song too?" Karima asked, noticing me when "Empty" came on. "I do the same thing." Karima and I bounced together as if performing a routine from the music video, though Janet hadn't made one for that song. Smiling and dancing, I looked at Karima. We were the same. Then, I considered that her room was likely the only place Karima could make such movements. I bounced a little lower, swayed a little tighter, and stepped a little lighter. We were different.

After we giggled and chit-chatted through getting dressed and wrapping khimars, it was time to apply makeup. Karima and Zakiyah each stared into a mirror and put on full faces, brushing on foundation, blush, eyeshadow, mascara, and lipstick. Watching them transform, I wondered how they would avoid ruining their makeup when we performed wudu and had to wipe water over our faces.

"Your turn, Sufiya," Karima said, turning to me with the countenance of a grown woman, not the chubby college kid I knew her to be.

"Naw, that's OK. I don't wear makeup." The only thing I applied to my face with any regularity was lip gloss; I had all kinds. I usually started with a base of ChapStick and then glossed it over with the kind shaped like a tube of lipstick or the kind I had to squeeze out of a hole at the end or the kind that required me to stick my finger in a jar. But that was all. The only time I wore more than that was when I went to the club; then, in an attempt to look older, I stroked several coats of black mascara on my eyelashes until they stuck out like hairy caterpillars and painted rainbows of eyeshadow across my lids until they shone like sunlight through stained glass.

"Aww, come on. It's a special occasion. You can wear some this time. Just a little bit," Karima insisted.

"Yeah, it'll look nice," Zakiyah joined in.

"OK, OK. Just a little on the eyes." I lifted my chin with Karima's fingertips beneath it, closed my eyes, and surrendered my eyelids to her black eyeliner pencil. I opened them to reveal the exaggerated outline made famous by Queen Nefertiti. A hefty shadow clung to every curve and trailed off with a dainty curtsy at the corner, adding a theatrical flair to my face that, by itself, would have looked ridiculous. But somehow, paired with my body-concealing clothing and head-covering khimar, it looked appropriate. I felt that at Eid, I'd fit right in. Finally. It was time to leave.

"Let's make du'a before we go," Karima said, prompting Zakiyah and me to stop packing our purses and put down the coats we'd just picked up. We bowed our heads and raised our open palms. Karima led us in a brief Arabic prayer. Whatever she said, I prayed that Eid brought all the enlightenment to my quest to be Muslim that I hoped it would.

I'd never seen so many Muslims gathered in one place before. They blanketed the huge hall wearing fine fabrics, sparkly jewelry, and googobs of makeup. A persistent buzz of English, Arabic, Farsi, and other languages I was not as familiar with hung in the air. Everybody seemed to be in a good mood, and as I walked around, getting a lay of the land, I smiled at everyone I passed, just happy to be there. The hall was a large, bare rectangle without partitions or windows, a vacuum of time. Off to one side was a wide-open area for praying. Some elderly people and families with young children squatted there with legs tucked beneath their haunches, having seemingly already staked out their spaces for the day. Vendors lined every other bit of floorspace with tables displaying jewelry, Islamic clothing, prayer rugs, food, books, and more for sale. Lights flashed, music played, the aroma of freshly baked pastries beckoned passersby. This was where the young people milled about, checking out the goods, but much more each other, reminding me of summer days with my sister, trawling among the vendors of Grant's Tomb in New York, where both the merchandise and the men competed for our attention.

Beneath the murmurs of native tongues and the competing broadcasts of music up and down the flea market aisles, I could make out the adhan being played.

"*Allahu akbar, allahu akbar. Ashadu'an la illaha illa'Allah . . .*"

I scanned the crowd, prepared to watch everybody drop what they were doing and rush in unison to whatever bathrooms were available to make wudu and then beeline to the prayer area for salat. But most people did not move. The music did not stop. Where I was standing, some vendors reached behind or beneath their tables for prayer mats, which they would spread on the floor of their booth to pray; but many—women and men—did not flinch. Maybe it was so loud in this cavernous hall that they didn't hear, I thought.

"*Ashadu'ana Muhammadan rasul Allah . . .*"

No, the adhan was faint but recognizable.

"Shouldn't we head over to make wudu?" I asked Karima and Zakiyah, walking beside me. They turned to look at each other.

"Do you think we should go?" Zakiyah asked.

"Nah, let's skip this one," Karima answered. "We'll make it up at the next one."

Skip this one? I thought. But this is what I came for. And what reason did we have to skip it? I could stroll, look around, and be looked at in a mall. I wasn't on my cycle, and I knew my friends weren't either. Yes, the line for sinks in the ladies' room was ridiculously long for wudu before the last salat but I didn't mind that much. It was part of the experience. I could wait again. If it meant a chance to get closer to God or to fulfill my promise as a Muslim, I'd gladly wait again. Yet I said nothing, allowing that Karima, Zakiyah, and all the people not praying around us had more experience in being Muslim than I did. And if they were okay with ignoring the pillar of salat, maybe that was part of the experience too.

However, there and then, it was not a part I wanted. Annoyed, I felt the need to break away from Zakiyah and Karima.

"I'm thirsty," I told them, spotting a booth with a refrigerator full of bottled juices. "I'm going to get something to drink. Y'all go on ahead. I'll catch up."

As I waited in line, scanning the fridge for my favorite Everfresh flavor, I noticed one of the salesmen staring at me. He was thin, with dark olive skin, and had black hair with fat, loose curls framing his narrow face. He seemed to be in deep conversation with another man, in another language, yet he didn't take his eyes from me. It seemed that to him I was an apparition, elusive in his dreams but subdued, stationary, and slowly approaching him in real life. Abruptly, he broke off his conversation with the other man: "I'm sorry, I'm sorry. Excuse me."

He walked over to where I was standing at the counter with the same look of wonderment in his eyes. "Can I help you?"

"Yes, do you have Pineapple Mango Everfresh?"

He looked at me as if I'd just asked the meaning of life and said, "Are you Muslim?"

My heart jumped as I worried that my khimar had slipped from my head or my blouse had come unbuttoned in the middle of an Eid celebration. But I could feel my hijab tight around my forehead and a quick glance downward confirmed that all my buttons were in place. I was fully covered in the middle of an Eid celebration, so I answered his puzzling question with an awkward drawn out, "Yes."

"Are you married?"

"No," I said, feeling no reason to lie.

"Do you have a *murafaqa?*" he asked, looking around.

I wasn't sure what he'd said, and whatever it was, I didn't know what it meant. But I figured it was something like an escort: "No."

"Then can we exchange phone numbers?"

This was not what I came for. I'd come to Eid for a more communal feeling of completion and accomplishment following a successful Ramadan. I'd come to strengthen my relationship with Islam and God. And I had come to this booth to get a drink. Not to find a boyfriend.

"No," I said again, hoping my terse one-word answers would give him the picture.

"Well, can we exchange phone numbers to our imams?" The man was pushy.

"No. You're too old for me."

"How old are you?" he asked confidently, as if he already knew the answer.

"Eighteen," I said, parched. "How old are you?"

"I'm only about twice your age," he said, and I laughed that at thirty-six years old—or maybe older—he was unfazed about propositioning a teenager.

But I remained firm in my denial.

Finally, the scenes of our life together that flashed over his eyes when he first spotted me faded and a look of annoyance came over his face. He snatched a napkin from the counter and scrawled his name and phone number on it.

"You can call me if you want to," he sounded defeated and shoved the napkin in my direction. He clearly did not take disappointment well; *not the kind of guy I should date*, I thought.

Just to end our uncomfortable exchange, I took the napkin and stuffed it in my coat pocket. "Can I still have my juice?"

The man reached into the refrigerator and put a bottle of orange liquid on the counter. I handed him a dollar, picked up my juice, and without saying more, walked away.

As I did, I kept contemplating what would make him start the conversation the way he did: "Are you Muslim?" Wasn't it obvious? Not on a normal day, but that day, when I made a real effort to fit in, to be like everybody else, why was I still made to feel as if I did not belong?

And why, when I felt so close to Allah by myself, did I feel oceans and universes away while surrounded by all those Muslims? The spirit of Allah that filled me when I recited al-Fatihah or ran around the lake surrounded by nature seemed to be missing from the celebration in this windowless room where practicing Muslims didn't pray and strange men got upset when you didn't give them your number. Being there, I didn't understand any better what being Muslim meant than I had before. I couldn't help but feel let down. I was making a sincere effort, but what was it all for, I wondered, as I rejoined Karima and Zakiyah and told them what happened when I went to get a drink.

"Some guy just gave me his number."

"For real? Who?" they asked looking around in disbelief. "Is he cute? Are you gonna call him?"

As I sat on my bed in my pajamas that night, I got curious to see the name of the pushy but persistent man I'd rejected earlier. I hadn't bothered to ask before. I wasn't going to call him, I told myself, I just felt bad that I'd upset him and wanted to know who he was. I hopped down and went to the closet where I'd hung up my coat. I reached into the pocket but didn't feel the napkin he'd given me. Nothing but the smooth rayon lining was there. Had I imagined our encounter? I reached into the other pocket, then remembered that before my friends and I left the huge hall and got back on our chartered bus to return to campus, Zakiyah tripped and spilled soda on her shoe. Rushing to clean it off before it got sticky, I reached into my coat pocket for a tissue from the bunch I usually kept there for my runny nose in the winter cold. I must have handed her the napkin that the driven, determined man had given me.

Realizing what I was thinking, I figured that even though I hadn't felt His presence, perhaps Allah had been with me after all.

36

My Burden

FRIDAY AGAIN. I brush my teeth, shower, dress, and reach into the bottom dresser drawer for my headscarf. It is the brown of amber with triangles of emerald, narrow rectangles of topaz, and the sapphire spaced-out teeth of combs boldly adorning its surface. Fringes fly at the ends; obstacles to my modesty at first, but now a uniquely understated feature of my headscarf design. I have become expert at wrapping.

First, I lay a small square nylon scarf, which will go under the khimar, flat on my bed. I take one corner and fold it onto its opposite, making a triangle. I pick it up and place the long edge over my forehead. My hairline, sideburns, and tops of my ears disappear, and my thick, natural hair that, unbound, rises into an Afro, is in repose. Carefully in place, I knot the scarf at the back of my neck.

Next, I take the amber cloth, long enough to circle my waist twice, and fold it onto itself once. A smaller rectangle now, I spread it on my bed and make it, too, triangular, with a rectangular sliver of material left over on one end. Arms outstretched, I grab opposite corners of the triangle and lift it like birds' wings above my head; the long edge perches atop the nylon scarf, steadying itself where my hairline would be. I bring the edges together at the nape of my neck, twisting them into a cord of autumn colors—rust, gold, fading green, deep sea blue—that I wind in circles, around and around itself, into a bigger and fatter bun until there is nothing left but a wispy end to tuck into the folds.

In the mirror, I am transformed. I am the same person I was when I awoke, but in my headscarf, I feel disguised, like an alter ego. With my hair out, I am Clark Kent, mild-mannered, small-town boy raised by his parents to be normal and instilled with American values, but disconnected from and longing for connection to his alien heritage. With my hair covered, I am Superman, alien in a strange land, sole survivor of a bygone society, haunted by the parents he never had the chance to know, and trying to live out the purpose for which he understands he was sent to earth. I am both, perhaps one more than the other, but neither can be separated from who I am. The costumes associated with each of my identities do not make one any less or more real than the other.

Properly covered, I go downstairs and head out the dorm and up the hill toward the Carnegie Building for jummah. It is weeks after Eid. The campus is warming up, thawing out. People are outside again. I slink past them, too far on the edge of the Yard for anyone to notice. Even still I wonder: If face-to-face, who will see me? Who will not? Who will look upon me and still be unable to identify me—or with me? Because of how I'm dressed, who will deny my humanity and simply label me alien?

I climb the stairs of the small, squarish building and kick my shoes into the pile inside the vestibule. I take a seat in the back of the room. Despite the disappointments of Ramadan and Eid, I am here like a dutiful Muslim. No one at the Eid hall, on this campus, or in this room may understand why I persist. What it is that I'm after, they may not know. When it is time for salat, I go for it. I refuse to just go through the motions, standing, bowing, and prostrating myself like the mechanical movements of an assembly line. I put heart into each posture; I seek connection with Allah in each position.

My experience may be taking place here in this room, but my consciousness yearns to be elsewhere; I focus on transcending my circumstance. From aloft, in the firmament, I look down and see myself kneeling on the carpeted floor, still and small. Billowing clouds silhouetted by golden sunshine surround and fill me with a sense of peace and comfort at my closeness to the Creator. Here, He is just over my shoulder, I am sure. But the shoulder of the woman beside me brushes mine, and I am back on the floor, ready to rise skyward again. The imam speaks, and I am totally earthbound.

"Some of you aren't displaying proper hijab," he starts, and I sink further into the floor, anticipating where this talk will go. "As a reminder, there are to be no words or images of living beings, human or animal, on your clothing or, sisters, on your khimars. Nothing to rival the worship of Allah, subhana wa ta'ala."

Good, I think, *I haven't violated any of those rules. So far, so good.*

"And don't forget, it is not only the sisters who are tasked with covering, out of respect for Allah, subhana wa ta'ala. Brothers, you are to cover your heads too, as the Prophet Muhammad, may peace be upon him, had demonstrated."

All right, safe again, I think, relieved to hear the imam focusing a lesson about attire on men.

"But sisters, the Holy Qur'an states that you are to guard your modesty: 'And say to the believing women that they should lower their gaze and guard their modesty.' If you believe, the Qur'an states, if you are a believing woman, then you will show it by obeying Allah's command. Lower your gaze and guard your modesty. You don't walk around with improper hijab, or no hijab, from Saturday to Thursday, and then come up in here covered only on Friday. We're not Christian and this isn't church. We don't play that game."

People chuckle and nod their heads softly. I am silent and still. The imam is making the whole masjid laugh—at me—though they don't know it. They see me only on Fridays. I've seen the imam outside of jummah; I've passed him with a smile, eye contact, and a nod on the street and around campus. Me, in T-shirt and jeans. He, in buba and kufi. I did not lower my gaze. I did not guard my modesty. I am a modern woman; I have no reason to hide, I thought, naïvely.

"For Muslim women, it is inappropriate for the bosom or the neck to be exposed," he continues, and I follow his gaze, waiting for his eyes to fall on me and reveal, this time to the entire masjid, that it is me he's talking about. My neck is visible today, as it usually is. "Again, sisters, it is the Holy Qur'an that prescribes 'that they should not display their beauty and ornaments except what must ordinarily appear thereof; that they should draw their veils over their bosoms and not display their beauty except to their husbands, their fathers,' and so on. This is the burden of the Muslim woman. This is what you must do if you believe. If you don't believe in the oneness of Allah, subhana wa ta'ala, then you can go out, bare necked, baring your bosoms, and do whatever you please. But, if you are a believing woman, if you do believe, then this is what God prescribes for you."

No one had admonished me about my neck before. I thought I was just being different; I didn't realize I was doing anything wrong.

The imam continues, and I wait with my heart roasting in my chest for him to point straight at me or call my name, exposing me, in front of everyone, as some kind of fraud. He never does. He ends his khutbah, and I try to believe that maybe no one but he and I know it was directed at me. But he and I might as well be everyone. Humiliation flushes my face and a knot lodges itself in my throat.

I've tried to shake the feeling of illegitimacy that's shrouded me and my various attempts to get closer to Islam, my birthright, but here it is again. Nothing I do makes it go away.

Though I was born of this other world and cast from it not of my own design, the imam seems to be saying that if I want to lay my claim and be Superman, I can no longer be Clark Kent. But I am Clark Kent. And sometimes, I am Superman. If I can't be the person my parents raised me to be and am apparently doing a terrible job being the person I was born to be, then, I wonder, who am I supposed to be?

When the khutbah ends, I get up from the floor, walk to the vestibule with my head down, and try to get my shoes on without having to talk to anyone. I'm holding myself together for now but don't know how long I can. I have to leave. Looking out the door, I can see the imam already standing on the stairs, greeting congregants as they depart to go about their days. But I have to leave. I'll be a puddle of tears if I try to wait for him to abandon his post before I go. I'll have to pass him. I have to leave now. I push through the door in a hurry, and when he sees me, he says, "As-salaamu'alaikum, sister."

I smile faintly but say nothing. Unable to speak or look him in the eye, this time, I lower my gaze.

I train my eyes, which are beginning to water, on the concrete steps I am bounding down and then on the pebble-filled path leading back to my dorm. I cross the street and, as I weep, finally begin to lift my head. It is a beautiful day outside, blue sky, intermittent sun, warm air with a brisk breeze. Nearing Founder's Library, I slow my gait to take in nature's beauty and notice the sudden tightness of my headwrap around my head. It is strangling me. I do not wait to get back to my room; I reach behind my head, grab the end of the wrap I tucked into the bun at the nape of my neck, and begin to unwind as I walk, around and around, looser and longer until the coils become a cord. I am in front of the library, within view of the imam if he's watching, when I finish unraveling. The pressure in my head subsides. I do not look back. I pull the cord into cloth—amber, emerald, topaz, sapphire—and drape it loosely about my shoulders, not caring if a sudden breeze were to come and lift the burden away.

37

Darkness on the Horizon

MY FATHER SHOULD HAVE BEEN basking in the newlywed glow—having married just weeks earlier—but instead, he was so frustrated he couldn't stop raving: no one respected Islam. No one understood Muslims. Muslims were always the scapegoat, and they just allowed it. They needed to stop letting fanatics speak for them, he was telling his new wife.

He'd been reading the *New York Post* and stopped at an article about a black man around his age being indicted in Queens for murdering a Catholic priest. The priest had been counting cash from his church's Mother's Day collection plate when someone came in and shot and killed him. During his arraignment, the suspect, Allen King, said that was not his "true name. My name is Malik Allah," the article stated. He claimed to be a Muslim.

Fed up, my father was unable to sit quietly by while Islam got dragged through the mud. He put down the *Post*, grabbed a piece of paper, and began scratching out a letter to the mosque's newspaper, the *Western Sunrise*. Like a man hopelessly in love with the town floozy, he felt the need to justify his attraction to Islam and defend its honor.

"For far too long the public has been misinformed about Muslims and the religion of Islam," he wrote. Working off the assumption that the *Western Sunrise*'s readership was aware that Islam did not advocate murder, including the murder of Christians, he thought of another way to expose the suspect in the priest's killing as a fraud: "Any Sunni (orthodox) Muslim knows or should know that the Islamic nomenclature does not permit one to assume for himself the name Allah or any of the 99 divine attributes of Allah without prefixing it with a form of the word *abdu* (servant of)." He added that "only Allah possesses these maximal qualities."

Pleased with the soundness of his argument, my father closed his letter, published in June 1973: "I pray that *The Western Sunrise* and the Mosque of Islamic Brotherhood will continue in their efforts to present to the people the truth of Islam."

A couple of years earlier, it would've been fair to say that my father believed in the Mosque of Islamic Brotherhood wholeheartedly. Under Imam Tawfiq's leadership, it was growing into an actual presence in New York City. It owned a couple of businesses in Harlem: Banu-Hilal Food Store, a health-food market at 665 Lenox Avenue that my father began managing soon after its opening; and Banu-Hilal Restaurant at 183 Lenox Avenue, a full-service, sit-down eatery, where many of the brothers were assigned to work as cooks, waitstaff, busboys, night security, and cleaning crew. Monthly, the mosque published the *Western Sunrise*, a newspaper that carried transcripts of Tawfiq's recent khutbahs, listings of prayer times, and articles of interest to Muslims and blacks alike written by MIB members, including my father. The mosque even offered its own MIB marriage certificates, divorce decrees, and certificates of name change; in my father's eyes, the Mosque of Islamic Brotherhood was bringing to life the self-sufficient Islamic society that once only existed in his dreams and among the newspaper illustrations pasted on his old bedroom wall.

After a year or so of bearing witness to Imam Tawfiq's efforts to make MIB an integral factor in the community—and not just a congregation of black Muslims—my father's hopes for the mosque soared. He believed, he would later tell me, it "would become a model to attract black people to an alternative lifestyle that was true in its religious orthodoxy and as valid as Christianity, Judaism, or anything else." He believed the mosque would achieve presence and stature not only in New York but nationally.

The problem, however, continued to be that MIB lacked a masjid, an actual physical structure where the congregants could assemble and pray. They had outgrown Tawfiq's apartment on Howard Avenue. And the International Muslim Society at 303 West 125th Street, where Tawfiq often gave khutbahs and where my father had first met him, was never really their home. At the time, they were still using Black Seeds, the St. Nicholas project community room, for jummahs.

"We're like nomads. A mosque without a home," Tawfiq told my father and a couple other brothers one day, citing the source of the name of the mosque businesses, Banu-Hilal. In the eleventh century, the Banu Hilal tribe had been a group of nomadic Bedouins who conquered areas across North Africa and ruled for one hundred years. Although eventually defeated by a Moroccan dynasty, the large and mighty tribe was the subject of epic poems, orally passed down throughout the Arab world by individuals and small groups of survivors for generations. They were given credit for the spread of Islam across the Sahara region. But, Tawfiq continued, "We should have our own building, uptown. It should be someplace prominent, someplace visible." Such visibility could attract more brothers and sisters to Islam, he said, and having a proper masjid to worship in would please those brothers and sisters already committed to MIB.

But as the years went by, there was still no masjid. And the only people who seemed to know about the mosque's health-food store, tearoom, and restaurant were mosque members or living right there in Harlem. Someone needed to spread the word, my father thought, about the goodness of Islam.

He didn't know what good his letter would do, if any. But he was compelled to say something because, for about the past year, he felt as though his faith were under attack. The onslaught began in April 1972, when MIB members, whom Imam Tawfiq had from the beginning instilled with a sense of community and a spirit of brotherhood, were confronted with the quandary of whether to act on it.

It was a Friday afternoon and the Nation of Islam's Muhammad's Mosque No. 7 was packed with hundreds of worshippers and students attending school, as usual. The mosque, then led by Min. Louis Farrakhan and formerly the home temple of Malcolm X, was always a lively place. In the midst of this, two plainclothes police officers burst in, responding, they said, to what dispatch told them was a call of an officer in distress at that address.

No one there had called the cops, Mosque No. 7 members told the two.

The officers, unconvinced, tried to take a look around.

Mosque members, offended by the police's presence inside their house of worship, surrounded them.

The officers called for backup. When more police arrived, they and mosque members tussled. The police, refusing to leave, argued their right to be there, while worshippers, trying to push them out, stressed their need to protect the sanctity of their mosque and the people in it.

Eventually, the worshippers forced out all but a handful of cops, including Officer Philip Cardillo, one of the original two, whom they then held inside the mosque. Somehow, during this detention, Cardillo was shot with his own gun.

"Shots fired. Shots fired," an officer radioed. Once that call went out, police converged around the mosque in droves.

Community members, including some from MIB, whose Banu-Hilal Restaurant was just three blocks from the Nation of Islam mosque, witnessed the show of force and responded in kind. Brothers from MIB, but not my father, chose to stand guard at Mosque No. 7 in an effort to protect hundreds of its worshippers still barricaded inside. Neighborhood residents, offended by the battalion of police invading their block, threw bricks and bottles, overturned a car, and assaulted white bystanders.

Meanwhile, police inside questioned more than a dozen suspects in the mosque's basement, trying to determine who had beaten and wounded their officers. However, with tensions on the street rising, after three hours they decided to end the near riot by releasing the suspects and withdrawing from the mosque. Cardillo had to be carried outside, dragged through the hostile crowd in the arms of a uniformed officer while surrounded by plainclothes cops with guns drawn. Six days later, Cardillo died from his wounds. No one was immediately charged with his killing.

Two months later, in June, while Imam Tawfiq gave a talk at Columbia University about Islam and nationalism, he defended MIB's decision to stand with Mosque No. 7 that day.

But didn't that suggest a "secret alliance" between the Mosque of Islamic Brotherhood and the Nation of Islam, an audience member asked, accusing Tawfiq. Such a claim was seen as an insult in the Sunni Muslim community. Between the religious beliefs of Muslims, there existed a wide chasm: Elijah Muhammad's followers sat on one side and followers of orthodox Islam, scores of whom had accepted it after Malcolm X denounced Elijah Muhammad, sat on the other. Many people did not see the bridge connecting the two. Tawfiq did.

"If that had been a church, we would have been there as well," Tawfiq answered, reflecting my father's own fond memories of the church, his initial reluctance to give up the cross he used to wear around his neck, and his rejoicing upon discovering Islam's acceptance of Christianity as a forerunner. "And if our accusers don't feel this way, then their Islam must be very narrow."

About a week after those comments, the Black Seeds Cultural Center that MIB was using as its mosque was vandalized, athletic equipment was stolen, and the charity box was broken into. Two weeks later, on July 2, with ten MIB members inside, a plastic bomb exploded in Black Seeds. No one was hurt, but to my father, these incidents spoke to the Mosque of Islamic Brotherhood's need to get its own masjid. It needed to do more to establish itself as a viable presence in the community, more to be recognized as a local beacon of Islamic righteousness.

The public readily believed that Muslims were suspected murderers, my father asserted, because there was nothing of note in the public sphere challenging that image. MIB brothers helped protect the Nation of Islam's mosque when it was compromised, but more than anything, they needed an opportunity to build and protect their own.

"I brought myself to this to be a part of something that I felt was larger than me," my father complained to my mother when all the bad news kept piling up, and there were no new MIB businesses to speak of and no masjid in the works and no sunlight on the horizon on which to train his eyes during the arduous journey to black upliftment. "But if I'm the spearhead of everything, then I've aligned myself with something that's not what I thought it was."

38

We Wouldn't Be Here

(

THE FIRST MONTH of the new year, 1974, was drawing to a close and it seemed to my father that in the Mosque of Islamic Brotherhood, nothing had changed. There was still no mosque, no real plans to get one, and no new brick-and-mortar accomplishments that he could count as progress. Surrounded by other patrons and sitting across from his friend Rashid at a table in Banu-Hilal Restaurant, he vented his frustration.

"I just don't see where all of our commitment and sacrifice is going. We all are broke. We all could be doing more for our families," my father complained. He had two little boys to feed and clothe, an ex-wife to support, a new wife to provide for, and another baby on the way. He could barely make ends meet as an electrical apprentice but was still expected to sell his monthly quota of the *Western Sunrise*; wash dishes, bus tables, provide security, or wait on customers at Banu-Hilal Restaurant; attend weekly Brotherhood meetings, pay monthly dues; give new converts their shahada, and more. He'd done all this willingly, joyfully, but it had worn him down. He was ready to stop. "I just don't see that our leadership is doing all that it can do. How much can we continually give and not see growth?" my father asked, making no attempt to lower his voice or temper his outrage, despite being in the company of other MIB members.

Most of the restaurant-goers ignored him. But two approached. They were tall, serious, and a bit older than him; my father recognized them as Attallah Ayyubi and Taha Abdullahi, two well-respected MIB brothers who were like right-hand men, almost bodyguards, to Imam Tawfiq.

"Brother, if this wasn't right, then we wouldn't be here," said Ayyubi, whose tone of voice reminded my father of Malcolm X. Ayyubi and Abdullahi had both been members of the Nation of Islam who, following Malcolm's split with the organization, joined his Muslim Mosque, Inc. After it disintegrated, they joined a fledging MIB, where, apparently, they intended to stay.

They were the kind of brothers my father looked up to. The kind that made him think that if he'd been a bit older himself and discovered Islam earlier, he might have also rubbed shoulders with Malcolm X. But at this point, not even brothers who reminded him of Malcolm, his hero, could do much to sway my father. His mind was made up. He decided that he'd had enough, and his time in MIB was over.

―――――――――――

A week later, on Tuesday, Feb. 5, 1974, my father got up early and headed to his electrical job in the Bronx. He was getting pretty used to the routine, although the money was not great, and with my mother six months pregnant with my sister, he'd taken on driving a cab after work to help make ends meet. When it was time for a coffee break, he went to the break area, sat among the day's newspapers his coworkers had left scattered around the room, and picked one up.

"B'KLYN MUSLIMS WAR; 4 SLAIN," he saw splayed across the front page of the *Daily News*. Below the headline was a photograph of what my father recognized as the entrance to Yasin Mosque in Brooklyn. He'd been there before. Painted in white above the front door was the shahada, "There is no God but Allah and Muhammad is His Prophet," written in Arabic script and then repeated below it in English. Two uniformed police officers stood in the light of the entryway and behind them, just visible through the legs of one of the officers, was a dead body on the floor of the mosque.

My father's heart began to palpitate; his breathing became shallow and labored.

How could this have happened? he asked himself.

At the most recent Brotherhood meeting he'd gone to, he heard that

Imam Tawfiq and a few MIB brothers planned to meet with Yasin. But he thought it was just to settle a tiff about Yasin's magazine's reprinting a portion of an article from the *Western Sunrise* without permission. Apparently, the article made reference to black people as Kushites, and MIB wanted credit for the reference. It was so trivial that he'd hardly thought anything of it.

"Police blame incident on war between competing Muslim factions," a sentence on the *Daily News*'s front page read.

It didn't make sense that such a small disagreement could have grown so out of hand, my father thought. He turned to the story inside:

> Police said that five gunmen, armed with shotguns and automatic pistols, burst into the Ya Sin Mosque at 52 Herkimer Place shortly before 11 p.m. and sprayed gunfire into a group of people. Two of the invaders were shot to death by Muslims in the mosque, police said.

The article named, incorrectly, the two men killed from Yasin Mosque. It did not name the other two killed and made no mention of the Mosque of Islamic Brotherhood.

But my father had a terrible feeling that MIB was involved.

He kept reading to the end of the article as it detailed seemingly unrelated recent tragic events involving Muslims and members of the Nation of Islam from New Jersey to Washington, DC. The paper called it "a growing conflict." Beside the article was another photograph, this one inside Yasin, in which a second body lay motionless on the mosque floor, police investigators in motion around it.

My father stared at the scene as a wave of confusion and anger swept over him. Yasin Mosque was part of Dar-ul Islam, the "house of peace," he remembered. Founded in 1962 by Sheikh Daoud Ahmad Faisal, the Dar—as it was commonly called—aimed to create a community of Muslims who lived according to divine law, as the Prophet Muhammad and his small group of followers had more than six hundred years earlier. Though its membership was intentionally black, blackness, nationalism, and political activism were downplayed in favor of thorough knowledge of and adherence to Islamic religious practice. Dar ul-Islam first occupied a mosque on State Street in downtown Brooklyn and by 1970 had established the Yasin Mosque on Herkimer Place in the Bedford-Stuyvesant neighborhood.

Yasin quickly became a visible and audible part of that community. Every day, five times a day, the mosque amplified the adhan over loudspeakers and opened its doors for prayer. Hundreds of young Muslims regularly crowded the three-story brick building. Gradually, the Dar opened several enterprises: an incense manufacturing and distribution business, a day-care center, a halal butcher, and a magazine called *Al-Jihadul Akbar*, the Greatest Struggle. The *Western Sunrise*, in a show of solidarity, featured some of these ventures in photographs and articles within its pages.

At Sheikh Daoud's urging, the Dar sought to emulate Yasin's success in Brooklyn in urban communities around the country. The vision was to carve out places where African American Muslims could practice their deen uninhibited. Proselytizing teams traveled nationally and soon formed Dar ul-Islam branches in more than a dozen cities, including Atlanta, Boston, Cleveland, Dallas, Los Angeles, and Philadelphia. At its height, the Dar had affiliates in forty-four US cities, all taking cues from its Brooklyn-based imam, Yahya Abdul Karim, and its main mosque, Yasin.

And four Muslims had been shot dead within its walls. Tears began to fill my father's eyes.

He got up, fled from the break room, and, without saying anything to anyone, stormed off the job. He was working not too far from Tawfiq's Bronx apartment, MIB's headquarters at that time. He walked straight there.

Still teary-eyed, my father started banging on the apartment door. He hoped that someone there could tell him what was going on and prayed that someone would say MIB was somehow not involved. He banged and waited and banged some more.

But no one answered the door.

Later that day, my father called over to headquarters and got someone on the phone. As he talked, he could hear voices in the background and knew that other brothers had also gone there to find out what happened.

He hung up and headed over to join them. There he found out, in no uncertain terms, that MIB was indeed involved.

Imam Tawfiq and a handful of his most trusted men acting as security had gone, armed, to Yasin Mosque for a meeting. Reportedly, the talk was to have something to do with conflicts that had arisen over whether and how to unite the disparate groups of African American Sunni Muslims that had been gaining traction around the country.

During a conference of Muslims in Philadelphia in 1972, Yusuf Muzaffaruddin Hamid of the Islamic Party in North America declared himself the leader of such an effort. But neither MIB nor the Dar, two of the other black mosques with strong leaders, were willing to comply with the plan. Hamid further angered both groups by claiming that Imam Tawfiq and another respected Muslim who worked within the black community were sympathetic to the Nation of Islam. Just like after the standoff with police outside the Nation's Mosque No. 7 in Harlem, Tawfiq's deen, and particularly the authenticity of his and all MIB members' Muslim faith, had been called into question.

Whatever dispute the meeting was supposed to solve, resolution never got off the ground. Different reports explain that when Tawfiq and his entourage arrived at the mosque, he was separated from them; he was escorted into the imam's office, while security was made to wait in the foyer. There were some raised voices both in the foyer and in the imam's office. Before anyone had a chance to ease the tensions, representatives from MIB and Yasin shot at each other, killing four and injuring at least one.

The injured was Jamil Abdul Haqq, a member of Yasin Mosque who was on desk duty, opening the mosque for visitors, that night. He was shot in the back and taken to Brooklyn Jewish Hospital. Despite immediate medical attention, he was left paralyzed from the waist down. Another Muslim man, who newspapers named and identified as a Harlem resident, denied to authorities that he was involved in the shooting but became a suspect when he checked himself into Harlem Hospital with gunshot wounds the same night. Police guarded him after a bullet the same caliber as one from the shooting was removed from his body but never arrested him after he recovered. An early member of MIB, he was the man who had performed my parents' wedding.

The dead were Bilal Abdullah Rahman and Muhammad Ahmed,

two amirs of Yasin Mosque, and two Bronx men who the *Daily News* identified the day after its front-page story as Peter Jeffreys and Edgar V. Mason. My father knew them as Attallah Ayyubi, 33, and Taha Abdul-lahi, the two men who had tried to dissuade him from leaving MIB in Banu-Hilal Restaurant the week before.

The *New York Times* reported that the injured Harlemite, Jeffreys, and Mason had all belonged to the Nation of Islam before joining "an African unity group established by Malcolm X." It said that all later became Sunni Muslims. It's unclear whether their affiliation with the Nation of Islam inadvertently, intentionally, or at all exacerbated tensions between the MIB group and the Yasin group that had met, unsuccessfully, attempting to unite African American Muslims that night.

What's clear is that although all the news stories immediately following the shooting attribute it to competing Muslim factions, none name the Mosque of Islamic Brotherhood as the other faction, and none say that Imam Tawfiq or Yasin's imam, Abdul Karim, were present. Members of both Muslim communities protected Abdul Karim, Tawfiq, and MIB. In crisis, the difference between these groups of Muslims was apparently not as important as what united them. Honoring a code of silence that both communities adhered to for years, MIB members and former members, including my father, remain tight-lipped about the incident to this day.

But the crisis could not be ignored. The shooting deaths of Muslims by Muslims was a tragedy of the highest order for MIB. And for my father, it was confirmation of his regard for the mosque finally hitting bottom. The uprightness, the brotherhood, the sense of empowerment that Tawfiq had instilled in him and members of MIB as Muslims and Kushites flew away from him like a balloon taken by a gust of wind. Having already made the decision to sever ties with MIB, and now learning that the brothers who said their presence in it signified its righteousness were themselves gone—and never coming back—my father saw no further reason to stick around.

39

The Search for Truth

☾

MY LEGS HAD HELD UP and carried me safely from the Carnegie Building to Frazier Hall after jummah. But as soon as I stepped off the elevator and approached my open dorm room door, my knees went weak, my chest began to heave, and I collapsed in sobs onto my bed. Fallen apart, I needed answers to put me back together. And I felt that my mother, who had withheld them from me thus far, was the one responsible for providing them. She needed to make sense of the mess I had gotten myself into. At the very least, she would provide comfort even if there was none to be had. I reached up for the telephone on my desk and dialed her number.

"Hello," she answered in her usual cheery tone.

"Hi, Ummi," I said, my voice weak and cracking.

"Uh-oh, what happened?"

Before I answered, I remembered my roommate crouched on her bed opposite mine and our door wide open, as usual. I didn't want anybody to see me crying, so I took the loose headwrap from my shoulders and draped its entire expanse over my head, face, and most of my curled-up body. Tented beneath my burden and choked up with tears, I whimpered and sobbed into the receiver, hoping my mother would understand the words that came between.

"Nothing makes sense anymore," I said. As a Muslim, it was my charge to follow the rules of what was halal, permitted, and what was haram, prohibited. But it seemed as if the more I learned about Islam, the more I realized that things I enjoyed—the things that made me, me—

were haram. Having a unique fashion sense, wearing hairstyles that conveyed personality, and dancing to a beat that literally moved me were all haram. "Now, I can't even show my neck anymore," I told her.

"Who told you that?" she asked.

"The imam," I answered. It was beginning to occur to me that if I wanted to start being a true practicing Muslim, I'd have to stop being myself. And I wanted to be both: I wanted to be the girl who found kinship with Malcolm X and comfort in prayer, the girl who identified God in nature and cried for Salim, the girl who fasted all day and still danced to Mobb Deep at night.

I begged Ummi to tell me I could.

"Can you please explain halal and haram again?" I asked, hoping I'd misunderstood something and could figure out that it was, indeed, possible to be the self I had grown up to be, Clark Kent, and the self I was born to be, Superman. I'd thought that the legacy of the African American Muslim was mine to claim. And because I already knew how and had no choice but to be black, knowledge of Islam had been the only thing preventing me from laying my claim. But now, it felt as if someone had placed my inheritance on a high shelf and left me no ladder to reach it. It seemed as though my only choices were to abandon it or make the whole thing come crashing down.

"I knew this would happen. This is what I was afraid of," Ummi said.

Hearing that made me cry more.

"I had some of the same problems when I was involved with the mosque, Feeya." Ummi told me about feeling like an outsider and about some of the sisters in MIB being cold to her. "So I chose not to be a very active member. I studied and practiced Islam mostly on my own," she said, and I wished she had told me that before. She went on: "Islam is a beautiful religion, but some people's interpretation of it can make it seem ugly. You can't let those people get between you and your Islam."

The more Ummi said, the more I cried. I shuddered and heaved, feeling as illegitimate as I did the day Aliya forced me to confront the fact that our parents had never been married. Still, with my voice broken and quaking, I tried to speak, concerned more with getting the answers that had eluded me for so long than that I was worrying everyone who passed by my door. My roommate and several of my floormates came up to me, trying to penetrate my makeshift tent to figure out what was wrong. But I wouldn't let them. My mother had set me up for this breakdown, and she was the only one I'd let help me through it. She seemed to be running out of things to say and began falling on her tried-and-true optimistic overtures: "You're doing the right thing, Feeya. Everything's going to be all right. Whatever you decide to do, it will turn out fine, OK? Don't worry so much about what other people are doing or saying."

The platitudes somehow soothed me, and my tears finally started to subside. That's when Ummi said something that immediately struck me as a truism I could not easily brush aside: "You gotta do things that make you smile."

It was simple, but it made sense. No one else was going to find happiness for me. I had to do that myself. Why was I letting someone else define what made me happy? Why did I allow someone to essentially wipe the smile off my face and replace it with the pained expression I was at that moment hiding from even my friends? I knew the things that brought me joy, and to deny myself those things just to live up to somebody else's ideal of what being Muslim was would be to deny my own happiness. That was nonsensical.

"Thanks, Ummi," I managed to say, slowly finding my voice again. My mother had indeed put me back together. Ready now to get off the phone, I felt confident that I knew right from wrong intuitively. As long as I was still smiling, I would know I was doing the right thing. "I'll talk to you later."

I lifted the veil from my face, got up from my bed, and began to let my friends know I was all right.

Until the very next day, when I fell apart again. My confusion returned because doing things that made me smile seemed like good advice, but I wondered what would happen if I was smiling at all the wrong times? I figured that an ax murderer probably takes pleasure in ax murdering, so if that's what makes him smile, should he do it? I didn't know what to think. I decided it was time to call Abi. Maybe his preoccupation with knowing all answers would serve me well this time. After a couple of rings, he picked up.

"Feeya. I'm glad you called." He answered the phone as if he'd been expecting me. I didn't know what for, though. I could hear the TV on in the background, and immediately, without listening to what I wanted, Abi started a conversation about the news story he was watching. It dealt with politics and Islam, his favorite subjects. Some kind of disagreement within the international Islamic community was upsetting him. A cleric in Yemen was mad at one in Saudi Arabia, who had a feud with another in Turkey over some Islamic jurisprudence, or something of that nature.

"These fools don't know what they're talking about," he said about the experts gathered to discuss the issue on CNN. But, of course, Abi did. He felt compelled to explain his view to someone, and I was as good a person as any. I readied myself for an hour-long conversation in which Abi did all the talking before either of us remembered that I was the one who'd called with something to say.

He turned his attention back to the international Muslims. "Each one of them thinks that he's the right one, and no one is willing to *listen* to the other." Abi's voice took on that worked-up high pitch that I now only heard while he was yelling at the people on CNN or relaying a story to me about the poorly mannered teens he called knuckleheads that he encountered on the subway or in his neighborhood in Harlem, where he moved after I graduated high school and no longer needed his address. "No one can admit that maybe the other guy, 'Hey, he might have a point there,'" he said, his voice turning into an Eddie Murphy character's before he laughed at his own joke. "You follow me?"

"Yeah, but maybe that's because they're trying to get the other guy to see the issue their way."

"Ah, yes. That's a good point. That's a very good point. But let me explain it another way," Abi said. "You see, if you had an object, any object, of a certain size and shape, and you placed that object in the center of a circle and you put people in different positions, distances, and vantage points around that circle and asked them to describe the object, everyone would say something different. Right?"

"Yeah," I answered tentatively, trying to avoid being roped in to agreeing with something I'd find out later I actually disagreed with.

"One person might say they see a circle and another person might say they see a sphere and someone else with an obstructed view might say they see a cone or a semicircle and so on and so on. Each person can only say what they see from their vantage point, their perspective. And no one can see the whole thing," Abi said. "Everybody wants to be the one with the one true answer, but everyone is right. And no one is right. You see, Feeya? Everyone's searching for truth, but there is no one truth."

It was very clever. Abi had known exactly what he would tell me to comfort me from the moment his phone rang and he saw my number on the caller ID. Ummi must've alerted him about my crisis. They were prone to do that now: talk to each other civilly when one of their children's well-being was in jeopardy. It was nice to see them working as a team. And I felt reassured, knowing that Abi had given my dilemma some forethought, but that he waited until I came to him to share his view.

He went on to explain that he and my mother had been attracted to Islam when they were younger and searching for truth. "When we were coming up, young people like us were looking for ways to better ourselves and our communities. And we had organizations in place dedicated to that effort. So, depending on our outlook and temperament, some of us joined the Black Panther Party, some got involved with the Nation of Islam, and others became part of Black Nationalist organizations or other groups. For your mother and I, Islam was the answer.

"Though I know you want to come to a similar conclusion in your experience, Feeya, within your own generation, no one is saying that Islam is the answer for you. And no one is saying that it isn't. Your mother and I raised you and your siblings to believe—or not believe—in whatever you choose," Abi said, and there it was again, that familiar refrain that left me wondering what had inspired it and, in some respects, led me on my search in the first place. "And as long as you're making an informed decision, we'll support whatever decision you make." He urged me to continue my search in earnest: "Everyone has to find their own truth, Feeya. You've got to find your own Feeya-ism."

It was essentially the same message Ummi had given me the day before. But hearing it from Abi was like listening with new ears. I may have been choked with emotion, but a newfound strength pumped in my chest and sent waves of confidence flowing through my body. I hung up the phone delivered from my wandering and onto a clear path. I now had a mission to find the truth, my truth. It was a mission I felt I had embarked upon long ago and, with my parents' blessing, had finally gathered the wherewithal to complete.

Figuring out how to be true to myself, I'd later learn, would be the easy part; discovering the truth of the legacy I carried within me, however, would prove more difficult.

PART IV

40

Being Black and Muslim

MY SEARCH EVENTUALLY led me back to Abi. But first I graduated from college and began working as a newspaper reporter a week after Muslim terrorists crashed planes into the World Trade Center. And wrote newspaper and magazine articles that explored Islamic practice and culture. And toyed with the idea of becoming a religion reporter. And for the first time in my adult life, allowed myself to write about myself. And didn't hate it. Actually, I kind of liked it. And I thought that the second-generation Muslim thing was a story—maybe not my story—but a story I needed to tell.

And that's how I got back to Abi, two weeks into my MFA program, at thirty years old, emboldened with a sense of purpose, but still terrified of my father's wrath.

"I want to do a project on what it's like to be a second-generation black Muslim," I blurted out, with an awkward smile spreading across my face as Abi and I sat in a tiny restaurant a few blocks from his apartment in Harlem. "I feel like people like me, who were born Muslim, have a different sort of relationship with Islam than the people who converted," I said, noticing how obvious my revelation sounded almost as soon as the words escaped my mouth.

What I meant was I was ready to find the truth of the legacy my siblings and I had inherited. And like any heir locating her place on the family tree, I wanted to follow my roots through the soil, along the trunk, and up to the branches, to note why either flowers, leaves, needles, or pine cones sprouted.

"So what's it going to be, one of these I-don't-know-who-I-am things?" Abi asked, and I was reminded of his disdain for uncertainty. To him, it indicated ignorance, brought on by a lack of proper study, usually in favor of some shortcut or easy route. I quickly tried to give my idea the illusion of having more shape.

"Well, maybe one part of it, but no," I added with conviction, "not the whole thing." Before I completely lost him, I figured I'd better get to my real point. "But," I said with a self-conscious smirk again overtaking my face, "I need to get the history."

"What do you need to do that for?" Abi asked.

While he loved to reminisce about how different the black community was in his day—how righteous he and "the brothers" had been, how purpose driven, how united—he never wanted to reach out to them. In the years since he'd last been involved with the mosque, Abi kept in touch with just one friend from there, his best friend, who happened to live clear across the country in California. He, himself, however, lived just blocks away from where the mosque was located and in the same city as many of the men he once called his brothers but didn't talk to anymore.

I didn't quite understand Abi's reluctance to reconnect with that time in his life. I knew it had meant a lot to him. And yet he'd always been hesitant to revisit the period in any significant detail.

At a loss for how to convince him, I could only think of maxims: "Well, what do they say? 'You can't know where you're going unless you know where you came from'?"

Somehow, that worked. Abi actually started talking. I fumbled in my purse for my notebook and a pen.

"See, when I came in, it was like heaven to me. All my religious aspirations, political aspirations, cultural aspirations, it was all here. It was great," he said, with a glassy look in his eyes and a grin growing on his face. But his gaze quickly clouded over and his smile faded as he continued: "Then you just watch it all come apart." There, in his face and his voice, was the familiar hurt, the pain, I heard every time Abi told me he was Muslim, but I didn't have to be. That was what I knew I needed to find out more about.

41

Revelation

(

THE NEXT DAY, I began to think I'd have to tell Abi that I was the one doing the research. His phone calls seemed incessant. His brain was percolating with ideas and details from his past he'd just remembered. There was so much he wanted to share, and all of it right away, that I almost told him he needed to calm down. I wanted to say, "Just relax and let me handle it."

But I didn't. I was the one who'd asked for his help. It wouldn't have been right to cut him out of a process he clearly found exhilarating. The best way I could think of countering his continuous supply of information was to originate some of my own and present to him what I found. I went to bed Monday night determined to do just that.

On Tuesday morning, I went online at the Washington, DC, office of the magazine where I worked as a researcher to begin my own research process. My very first discovery about the Mosque of Islamic Brotherhood stunned me: "Another tragic incident occurred at the *Yasin Masjid* (a Darul Islam facility) in Brooklyn, NY, in 1974," I read from a paragraph buried toward the end of part two of a Muslim blogger's five-part series called, "Why Blackamerican Muslims Don't Stand for Justice?" Interested, I read on: "After a dispute a [*sic*] arose between MIB Imam, Tawfiq, and Yah Yah [*sic*] Abdul-Kareem, leader of the DAR, two MIB men drew weapons which led to the death of two brothers from the DAR."

I stared at my computer screen and read the words again: "[T]wo MIB men drew weapons which led to the death of two brothers from the DAR."

Confounded, I printed out all the related posts I could find and still could hardly believe what the article said. *Black American Muslims had purposely killed other black American Muslims? At a mosque? And the ones responsible belonged to the same mosque Abi belonged to, at the very same time? And he didn't tell me? Why didn't he tell me?*

Thinking about the implications, a din of shouts and accusations filled my head and made me dizzy. I questioned whether my father was involved or was part of the cover-up or was the perpetrator himself. But I reasoned it was just a blog, filled with typos and misspellings. *Maybe it isn't true.*

Quickly, though, I found a response to the series from Imam Talib Abdur-Rashid, MIB's imam, whom Abi had intended to introduce me to two days earlier. Imam Talib lauded the articles, but in one of his "points of feedback" regarding the "tragic conflict" offered the blogger and historian only this Taoist saying, which he attributed to Malcolm X: "Those who know don't say. Those who say don't know."

I knew then that however fuzzy the details might be, the main gist of what happened at Yasin Mosque back in 1974, when black American Muslims shot and killed their brethren, was absolutely true.

I stewed at my desk a couple hours, not wanting to call Abi and yell at him in the middle of the office but too upset to call him without yelling. That afternoon, once the passage of time had calmed me a bit, I got in my car, began circling the streets of Northwest DC, and took out my phone.

"Abi." My tone was no-nonsense when he picked up. "Why didn't you tell me this stuff about Yasin?"

"Uh-oh." He already sounded guilty.

"'Uh-oh,' what do you mean 'uh-oh'?" I chuckled, but I was furious. "Why didn't you tell me?"

"Tell you what? About the shooting?"

"Uh, yes, about the shooting. Your imam was involved in a murder, excuse me—two murders—and you don't think it's important to tell me

224

that?" I raised my voice then, outraged that my father knew exactly what I was talking about yet, somehow, had neglected to mention it.

All of a sudden, he was ready with his story.

"I didn't find out about the shooting myself until the day after it happened," he began. "I was working a job in the Bronx, and I saw something in the newspaper about a shootout at a mosque in Brooklyn I was familiar with. I had been there before, checked out their jummah, you know. Anyway, something about what happened told me it had something to do with MIB."

"What gave you that idea? Was your imam involved in shootings before?" I asked sardonically.

"No, Feeya. I don't remember why," he dismissed me. "But I called the mosque to find out what happened. And I found out that MIB had indeed been involved. So after work, I went to an apartment near where I was working in the Bronx where a lot of the brothers had gathered to get more information, and they told me what happened. There was a verbal altercation at the mosque, and security for each imam was protecting their leader. Both sides were armed, so they drew their guns, shot, and killed each other." Abi spoke patiently then, as if the measure of his words could somehow buffer for both me and himself the impact of such a calamity.

"So there were people killed on each side?"

"Yes, two brothers on security from each side."

"So four people in all?" The article had only mentioned two.

"Yes. It was an unfortunate and unnecessary escalation, a real tragedy." His words began to sound practiced, as if he'd been anticipating having to speak them for some time.

"And you weren't there?"

"No, I wasn't there." My father offered nothing more. And because he hadn't exactly been forthcoming with the little bit of information he gave me, I wasn't sure whether I believed him. I hung up the phone, upset and unsatisfied with what he'd said and what he hadn't.

By Thursday, two days after that conversation, my father's phone calls to me diminished to none. I thought he was avoiding me, not wanting to say any more about the shooting, hoping I'd let it alone. Either that, or he was giving me time to get over how mad I was at him. It wouldn't have been the first time.

I had no idea, however, that the reason I didn't hear from him was because an aneurysm that not even he had realized was lying dormant in his head—somewhat like the secret itself—had burst and, unbeknownst to everyone, traumatized him with bleeding on his brain. He'd passed out in his apartment, where no one knew he lay alone and unconscious for an entire day. Until something woke him and told him to call me.

42

My Fault

C

FOUR DAYS AFTER our conversation about Yasin Mosque, I finally got a call from Abi. It was a Saturday, a little after one in the afternoon. His voice was groggy with sleep and his speech a bit slurred.

"I sent you some, uh, DVDs about Malcolm X," he said. "The videos should help you . . . better understand . . . the leader . . . who laid the groundwork . . . for MIB," Abi said, his speech slow and garbled, as if talking with a mouth full of syrup. "Are you at work now?"

"No, I don't work there on the weekends," I explained, referring to my job at the magazine. Abi had long been in the habit of sending me packages there to make sure I actually got the daytime deliveries I usually missed at home.

"Well . . . maybe you can tell . . . your coworkers . . . to keep an eye out for it . . . for you."

"It's Saturday, Abi. No one's there."

Abi seemed confounded, almost embarrassed, as he explained that he hadn't forgotten what day it was but somehow had missed one completely.

"So you don't remember Friday at all?" I asked.

"The last thing I remember . . . is coming home on Thursday night."

I hung up the phone and immediately tried to get one of my siblings to go check on Abi. Talking to him on the phone was one thing, but seeing him would be another. I called my oldest brother, Idris, who lived just blocks away from Abi, but he was out of town. I called my second oldest brother, Aqil, who also lived in Harlem, but he didn't think anything was wrong. The next day, Sunday, I called Muhammad, my younger brother, who usually backed me up on my concerns but this time thought I was worried about nothing. Then, on Monday morning, after she spoke to Abi herself, at last, my sister, Aliya, agreed that something wasn't right and sent the one sibling I hadn't yet called to Abi's building.

As soon as Isa saw that Abi couldn't climb the single flight of stairs leading to his apartment without gripping the railing with both hands and pulling himself up rope-climber style, he called an ambulance. They rushed Abi to Harlem Hospital, then transferred him to Bellevue, which specializes in traumatic brain injury. From there, I heard the words that immediately brought tears to my eyes and ultimately brought me home: "Abi has a brain aneurysm," Aliya told me. "I think you should come up."

———————

My siblings, Ummi, and I had been camped in a tiny waiting room off Bellevue Hospital's emergency–intensive care unit awaiting news about Abi all day. Night had fallen and we were all tired. We wanted to go home, but no one would budge until the doctors—who'd been walking past us, whisking in and out without acknowledging our presence—told us what was going on. When one came out in his navy blue scrubs, carrying a backpack as if calling it a night, we stopped him.

"Excuse me," Ummi stood to get his attention, "but is somebody going to tell us something?"

We already knew that Abi had suffered a ruptured brain aneurysm that had been bleeding into his brain for days. It struck him during a salsa class he took on Thursday night and made him black out, alone in his apartment, on Friday. He could have died right then—simply not waking up—but somehow he came to on Saturday and picked up the phone.

When Abi first got to the hospital, doctors put a tube in his head to suck into a bag beside him the excess blood putting pressure on his brain. We wanted to know what they'd do next.

"We've been waiting here, and no one has told us a thing," Ummi said, chuckling a bit, nervously.

The doctor stepped over to the bank of multicolored fused plastic chairs, where we sat beside a sole metal-grated vending machine. He faced us and began to explain.

"Your father," he looked at my siblings and me for confirmation that he got the relationship right, "is being scheduled for a craniotomy. Doing a craniotomy on a ruptured aneurysm can result in sudden death," he said, with all the nonchalance of remarking that cloudy skies could lead to rain. "He could die on the operating table, or it's possible that he might suffer a stroke in the days following the surgery, which could kill him," he said, and I glared at him, incredulous at the man's overt lack of optimism. "There also could be blood clots on the brain, which again would create the possibility of sudden death. And even if he survives the operation," the doctor said, as if gearing up to deliver a final blow to the dead horse before him, "he could suffer brain damage, which would result in cognitive or memory loss." With that, he gripped the shoulder strap of his backpack a little tighter and left.

My mother, my siblings, and I all sank in our scooped plastic chairs, reluctantly releasing some of our effort to remain upbeat.

I had to believe that the doctor was just doing his professional duty, preparing the family for the worst, just in case the patient encountered it. But I reasoned that Abi would make it through the surgery; he was strong. He'd already survived four days with blood leaking into his brain. And even then, he was able to remember my project and mail me a package of DVDs about Malcolm X. Besides, if he didn't make it, I thought selfishly, who would guide me toward discovering the truth of the legacy I had inherited? Who would help me get closer to finding out what made me who I was? Who, besides me, would know that the stress Abi experienced after I brought up the Yasin shooting, forcing him to revisit memories he'd long ago tried to forget and heartbreak that may not have healed but perhaps had been adequately patched up—which, exposed, I wholeheartedly believed, led to the aneurysm's rupture and my father's near-death experience—who else would know that it was all my fault?

43

All That Was Left

(

AFTER THE SHOOTINGS at Yasin Mosque, several other families also began to quietly leave the Mosque of Islamic Brotherhood. Some moved to other boroughs or out of the city completely. Some couples divorced, and either one or both ended their affiliation with the mosque. Others found that MIB no longer fulfilled them spiritually or politically—or both—and moved on. By 1975, membership had fallen to around twenty families from about fifty to sixty at its height in 1972.

My father, confident that his MIB days were over, still had no plan for what he would do apart from the mosque. In the nearly four years he was with the mosque, he'd inflated himself with such high hopes for all MIB could be and tied its success to the betterment of black people nationwide that when those hopes faded, all the air flew out of him like an unknotted balloon.

He considered joining another mosque. He'd attended jummah services elsewhere before. He'd also visited Unitarian and other humanist churches, thinking their universalist outlooks would be something to which he could relate. But none of them felt right. They were just different houses of worship. My father hadn't joined MIB simply because he was looking for a place to pray. He'd been seeking a completely new way of life and, briefly, had found it with Tawfiq and his Mosque of Islamic Brotherhood.

With MIB, my father not only embraced the religion of Islam but was also surrounded by brothers willing to work as hard as he did in service of a goal; he was also encouraged to carry himself with the dignity of a Kushite; he was inspired by a grand vision of a better life. Without MIB, all that was left was the religion. Without the mosque's establishing itself as a visible presence in the black community or working to provide the community with alternative moral venues; without the imam telling young inner-city blacks that they could be more than second-class citizens and do more than no good, what was the point of religiosity, he wondered?

He was still a Muslim, but Islam became something he internalized. His vision of what Islam could do through an organization like MIB became something he tried to forget.

Three months after my father parted ways with the mosque, my mother went into labor. It lasted for eighteen hours, and my father stayed with her the whole time, urging her to use the breathing techniques they'd learned in the Lamaze classes she'd made him sit through. Finally, my mother gave birth to their first child together, my father's first daughter. My sister, whom they named Aliya, "exalted one," was born in May 1974, five days after my parents' first wedding anniversary. My mother was nineteen years old. My father was twenty-three.

From the hospital, they brought Aliya to the tenement building on Woodycrest Avenue in the Bronx, where they lived in a roach-infested, one-bedroom apartment. My father, using his carpentry skills, did his best to make it a home. He had the floors stripped and varnished. In one of the kitchen cabinets, he built my mother a spice rack. At the edge of the kitchen, he installed a counter, partially held up by cinder blocks, where he and my mother could sit and eat. He'd painted the walls three different colors to resemble picture frames; brown paint framed a gold border against a beige background. On the ceilings, he tried to recreate a look he admired by applying a drywall compound, pulling at it to form a bumpy texture, and throwing metallic glitter up to the wet paint to make it sparkle as if it could be a starry afternoon. Using a projector, a transparency, and brown paint, he traced a pinwheel of Arabic calligraphy to decorate the living room wall. My father did everything he could think of to make the place more than what it was.

The apartment was not only their home, but with no consistent mosque to go to, it had become my father's main house of worship. He would make salat on his prayer rug right there in the living room, on a small piece of floor not already occupied by furniture or baby toys. This was his Islam.

He was in the middle of making salat one day about a year after the shootings at Yasin and his departure from MIB—a year after his world came crashing down—when my mother gathered her things, picked up nine-month-old Aliya, and prepared to take her for a walk. My mother, who dressed in hijab and was native to the Bronx, would approach other sisters she saw on the street with her warm smile and welcoming "As-salaamu'alaikum, sis," and managed to make friends with a few Mus-limahs in the area. This was her Islam.

On her way toward the front door to go outside, she walked in front of my father praying. Doing so was haram, interrupting the prayer was like my mother's coming between him and God, blocking the blessings. Before my mother reached the doorway, my father slapped her so hard she fell back in tears.

Shaken, her eyes flickered over the picture-frame walls and Arabic calligraphy. They drifted up to the stars sparkling overhead and settled on her husband's face distorted in anger. Later, regretting that he had hit her and no longer willing to stand by whatever justification he thought he had, my father fasted thirty days to repent, recognizing his own act as haram. Right then, however, shocked but not surprised, my mother got up. She grabbed baby Aliya and fled outside to the home of a friend. The friend did not have to ask why she had come. With one look, it was clear my mother was in trouble.

44

Wishing Him Well

UMMI WAS THERE AS ALWAYS. I hopped out of her car, slammed the door, and started running as I hadn't in years. Knees up, toes down; Abi had cautioned me against this posture many times while jogging around the lake. But it was nearly eight o'clock, the time he was scheduled to have his craniotomy at Bellevue, and Ummi, Aliya, and I had just found a parking spot several blocks away. We were late. We had to sprint.

Abi needed the craniotomy to repair the burst aneurysm in his head. It meant cutting into his scalp. It meant lifting the scalp from his skull so surgeons could saw into it and remove a bone flap. There, with the brain exposed, they'd be able to see the aneurysm. First, they'd drain excess fluid from around it, and next, once what they were looking for finally became clear, they could place a metal clip across the burst aneurysm to stop its bleeding. Then they'd replace the bone flap, suture Abi's scalp back together, and bandage him up. Of course, every step of the procedure carried its own risks. Every step could be my father's last.

"We have to make it in time!" I called back to my mother as I surged ahead, struggling to keep my feet in the too-big sandals she'd let me borrow because I didn't have time to pack before boarding a train from DC to get to New York. My heart pumped and my legs rotated like the rod connecting locomotive wheels, around and around with steam force against the gum-stained New York City sidewalks. With Aliya right behind me, I ran to be Abi's last dose of encouragement before he was forced into unconsciousness. I ran to see my father a final time before I might never see him again.

I stopped to catch my breath only when I reached Abi's floor. Already, a surgeon and nurse were rolling him on a gurney into the hallway as we walked up. We called out to them and they paused. Their hands gripped the metal railing surrounding each side of the bed Abi lay in, silent and motionless, a prisoner. His body was shrouded in a white sheet, his head partially obscured by the dressing that hid his drainage tube. Nearly half of his head and face had been shaved where the surgeons would need to make their incision to access the piece of skull they'd remove, I surmised. It was the first time I'd ever seen the flesh of Abi's cheek beneath his beard, the first time that symbol of him as a Muslim had been compromised.

Ummi and Aliya each took turns kissing Abi's cheek, wishing him well while the surgeon and nurse watched and waited to move on. I leaned over one of the bed's metal rails on my tiptoes last and kissed Abi's face. I hoped that the tears I felt welling up stayed in their place, and, for the moment, they did.

"Good luck," I said, steadying my voice. Looking into Abi's reddened eyes, wide and darting about as if searching for an escape, I realized I had never before seen my father so visibly shaken with doubt. He was terrified, although I could tell he was trying not to show it. I felt almost as stricken, temporarily masking my feelings of guilt for uncovering the long-forgotten mosque tragedy and forcing him to confront it. "We'll all be waiting for you when you get out," I told him, as the doctor and nurse began pushing his bed back down the corridor, with me walking alongside.

I wanted to add an "Insha'Allah" to remind Abi that even if none of his family could be, Allah would be with him in the operating room. But I thought the statement, God willing, would sound as if I doubted Abi's chances at survival. I didn't want to add uncertainty to an already precarious situation. I knew how much Abi would hate that.

Yet nothing else felt right. So I said it. And Abi repeated, "Insha'Allah," as his bed rolled ahead of me.

Then I could follow his path no further. I could only stand still and watch my father disappear down the wide and barren hallway.

45

History Holds Power

AS PROMISED, after the surgery, we were all there to greet Abi when he awoke. My mother, who despite her differences with him never even considered not coming, was there, as were Idris, Aqil, Aliya, Isa, Muhammad, and I.

One by one, we entered a holding area for patients just out of surgery but not yet assigned to recovery rooms. The area was partitioned into tiny cubicles. Each had barely enough space for a hospital bed, let alone a visitor. The partitions were made out of pale thin sheets. Voices of other visitors in adjacent cubicles, chatting with their loved ones in foreign languages and accented English, sounded so close I looked over my shoulder. Could Abi hear them, I wondered, as he lay in his bed looking weak and drowsy? No room for a chair, I stood before him holding his hand. The veins on the back were not as pronounced anymore; they still flowed, but thinner, weaker, older. I put my palm beneath his, allowing his head line, life line, fate line to radiate from my own. He could feel me, I believed, but would he know who I was? I didn't know what Abi remembered, if anything, and couldn't tell whether he was coherent or in possession of any of his faculties. But I wanted him to hear my voice.

"Hi, Abi. It's me, Feeya."

"Feeya," he groaned, more as my echo than out of any recognition.

I wasn't sure what to say next. When Abi and I spoke, which was often, we usually talked politics. He called whenever he saw something infuriating on the news and needed to vent. He called whenever he had a political theory he thought was clever and wanted to share. He would speak with passion, at length, and sometimes end the conversation with an apology for taking so much of my time and getting so worked up. But I couldn't bring up anything like that and stress his brain, which undoubtedly needed rest.

I remembered that Abi also liked to discuss movies he'd just seen. It was one of our frequent topics because he went to the theater every chance he got, although he was trying to cut back because it was getting so expensive. I decided to talk about a film.

"Me, Hummad, and Aqil just saw a movie," I started, sort of as a test to see whether Abi still had the capacity to understand me and to give me something to do besides stand there. "You wouldn't have liked it. It's called *District 9*, and it's supposed to take place in South Africa. But everyone there is white, except this bunch of Nigerians who are like organized criminals who sell guns and prostitutes out of this camp that aliens invade." I quickly realized that the subject matter of this particular film might not have been the best topic for recovery room conversation. "I don't know; it was dumb. Both Aqil and Hummad fell asleep on it," I said.

Abi could barely keep his eyes open while he listened. Based on his blinks and nods, though, he seemed to be trying to follow along with what I was saying. But I wasn't quite sure he was capable. Suddenly, he parted his dry mouth to speak: "You paid . . . twelve dollars . . . to see a racist movie?" he asked me in slow slurred speech.

I had to smile. "Yeah. I guess I did. All three of us did." With that, I knew Abi was the same, with his faculties, ethics, and memory of his latest campaign against rising movie ticket prices still in place. I laughed. My father was going to be all right.

Almost as soon as the nurses wheeled Abi's bed into a recovery room, he began receiving visitors. I had never before seen the people who came but knew immediately where they had come from.

The first was Abdullah Abdur-Razzaq. He was a stout man with a round belly, light brown complexion, scraggly salt-and-pepper beard, and a white crochet kufi on top of his head. When he waddled into my father's room carrying a bouquet of flowers and a bunch of bananas, Abi was wearing a sort of kufi too, which I hadn't seen him do in decades, but his was made of white gauze. Abi, lying at a forty-five-degree angle in the hospital bed, recognized the old man immediately.

"Ahki," he said, reaching out a weak hand for Abdullah to grasp, "As-salaamu'alaikum."

In 1967, Abdullah with Tawfiq had been one of the founders of the Mosque of Islamic Brotherhood. I'd learned the fact just days earlier, after Abi had given me his phone number. When I called, I found out that before he became a Sunni Muslim, Abdullah had been a member of the Nation of Islam and a close aide to Malcolm X. He'd also served as secretary of Muslim Mosque, Inc., the organization Malcolm X founded in March 1964, days after his contentious break with the Nation of Islam. And Abdullah had his heart broken at the Audubon Ballroom on February 21, 1965, when he witnessed Malcolm X shot to death.

This man was like a piece of living history, and he brought flowers and fruit to my father's bedside.

The next day, a man named Yahya Abdul-Hakim came. He was an electrician, like Abi, with a wiry frame and a midneck-length gray beard. He told me that Abi had been the one to give him his shahada to become a Muslim at MIB in the 1970s. Apparently, I discovered only then, Abi had some sort of a leadership role within the mosque. And yet, despite thanking Yahya for the poster he'd brought with the dates and times of fasting for that year's Ramadan, which had just begun, Abi hadn't observed the month himself in ages.

Then came a whole slew of brothers—Luqman Abdush-Shahid, who'd briefly been MIB's imam; Mustafa Abdul-Azim, MIB's well-respected Arabic teacher; and Salahuddin Abdur-Rahim, Abdur-Rahman Zaid, and Mikail Abdus-Samad, all early members of the masjid.

Where have they been all these years? I wondered.

I watched them crowd Abi's tiny hospital room and greet him as if it hadn't been thirty-five years since they were all acquainted, as if time hadn't dulled their youthful idealism and realigned their priorities. I listened to their laughter, prayers, and reminiscences bubbling up, filling the air and lifting Abi's spirits. I hadn't believed it before, but I saw then that Abi actually did have friends, once upon a time.

Would they have reconnected if Abi's life hadn't been in danger? Would they have come if I hadn't started asking questions and made Abi reach back to find some of them for me? I didn't know. But I saw that they acted more like brothers than a group of men he arbitrarily bestowed the honorary Muslim title upon. It seemed that no matter how long they'd been away from each other, because of the Mosque of Islamic Brotherhood they shared a bond that would always allow them to come together.

"My daughter is starting a project about MIB," Abi piped up as he became more comfortable with his company.

I smiled politely and noticed the suspicious smirks that came over their faces when some of the brothers asked, "Oh yeah?"

"Yeah, she's good," Abi continued. "She already asked me about Yasin."

A momentary panic seized me when I realized that not only did Abi remember the taboo subject I'd brought up with him, but now he was mentioning it to others, potentially inviting more danger.

"Yeah? What did you tell her?" asked one brother, whom I hadn't seen crack a smile yet.

"Nothing," Abi began. "I just said that there was a misunderstanding." But my gut told me that despite Abi's dismissive tone, the brother would not easily let the matter go.

To avoid being questioned about what I knew or riling Abi any further with talk of the tragedy, I used their spat as a diversion and slipped out the door. I was eager to discover the truth about the shooting and whatever else happened at MIB that, as Abi said, had made "it all come apart," but I would not do it in his recovery room. If I'd figured nothing else out within that week, I learned I had to be careful: History held power.

Instead, during the days, weeks, months, and years that followed, I gathered information about the transformative period in Ummi and Abi's lives when they became Muslim. I urged them to remember it, to unearth stashed-away photographs, documents, joys, and sorrows. I interviewed their friends and relatives, and read books, articles, and official paperwork from and about that time and on Islam. What I pieced together from this learned history not only revealed a more complete picture of my parents' experiences, ideologies, and identities, but the research forced me to realize, in ways I hadn't before considered, the impact their legacy has had on me. In looking back at their Muslim lives, and at the same time my own, I achieved a clarity about my inheritance that had eluded me for too long.

The author with her father at her sister's wedding.
Brooklyn, New York, 1998.

EPILOGUE

My Son

EXACTLY ONE YEAR after Abi's rebirth, on the anniversary of the day he ended his five-week stay in Bellevue hospital recovering from the brain aneurysm that nearly killed him, I gave birth to my first child. Labor lasted for twenty agonizing hours. My mother, who herself had birthed the four children she'd said she wanted, was there to rub my back while I walked the hospital's hallways in search of relief. My husband took with grace the criticisms I shot at him from my pain-filled chamber of annoyance. And as soothing Sade changed to bouncy Bob Marley on my birthing playlist, relief came—my son was born.

Almost as soon as the doctors in the Washington, DC, hospital put him on my chest and I saw the searching eyes and scrawny fingers only imagined in sonogram photos, Ummi's cell phone rang. It was Abi in New York. He wanted to know his grandson's name. My husband and I had chosen it maybe months before, but up until then hadn't revealed it to anyone.

"Samaadi Cabral Scott," we told Ummi, and she repeated to Abi.

My son would not be an Abdur-Rahman. But he was in my body for nine months and would hold a piece of my heart forever. I still wanted him to be a reflection of me, so after stumbling across the term in a book on Sufism, I chose Samaadi, my take on a Sanskrit word for one of the stages of enlightenment. Like Yogis, Sufis are always trying to attain a state of enlightenment. Having a child would probably be as close as I would come in my lifetime, I thought. Even if I never reached any state of awakening to ultimate truth—about the world, about human nature, about God—I hoped maybe Samaadi could. My first act as a parent was hoping my child would be greater than I could ever be.

My husband gave him the middle name Cabral, a completion of his own, Amilcar. Amilcar Cabral, who my husband was named after, was an African nationalist leader who fought and died for the independence of Guinea-Bissau from its colonizer, Portugal. My husband's first act as a parent was wishing strength for his child, for Samaadi to be a warrior against oppression, for freedom.

"What does it mean?" Ummi relayed Abi's question from the phone.

We explained our lofty reasoning and the historical significance, yet most of our words were façade. Publicly, my husband and I may have professed our desire for our son to be some enlightened revolutionary, but in reality, more than anything, we wanted the same thing all parents want of their children—the same thing my grandfather wanted of Robbie and my grandmother of Jody. It was the same thing Abi wanted when he named me and each of my siblings: We wanted our son to be an earthly extension of our best selves.

More than fifty years after its founding, the Mosque of Islamic Brotherhood is still around. Tucked away on its little Harlem side street in one of two apartment buildings the mosque purchased in 1977—the other, a brownstone, was condemned in the early 1980s—it survived. It survived the shedding of members in the mid-1970s; the shuttering of its businesses in the late 1970s; Harlem's crack era from around 1985 to 1995; the death of Imam Tawfiq at age fifty-two from Parkinson's disease in 1988; the period of adjustment to a new imam, Talib Abdur-Rashid; the September 11, 2001, terrorist attacks; and the aftermath of war with Muslim nations from 2001 to the present day.

The last time I saw Imam Talib, as he's familiarly called, he was presiding over a New York City ballroom full of people gathered to celebrate MIB's anniversary. He was sixty years old, the same age as my father then, and carried his age with a similar heft of frame, a familiar tinge of gray. At the time, he'd been leading the masjid for more than twenty years—balancing the weight of its impact and the width of its reach all on his own shoulders. Through him, the mosque had gained national recognition as a bastion of righteousness for African American Muslims.

"I would like to have the confidence that I could die and there'll still be an MIB for my grandchildren," he said in a documentary about MIB's founding that played during the celebration. He analogized his possible retirement to the handoff in a relay race, perhaps recollecting those weekend runs around New York City neighborhoods with Imam Tawfiq: "I want to pass the baton to the youth, but . . . the baton exchange, that's critical. You can take the baton and mess up the whole race."

What Imam Talib said as he stood at the podium later that night, in a flowing buba and tilted fez, was perhaps more telling of his thoughts about MIB's future. As he spoke to the audience of mature Muslims, decades into their deen, he admitted that an Islamic upbringing had been difficult for some of the first generation's children to bear.

"When you look at us and our sons and daughters," Imam Talib said, "you see some problems there. There is unhealed pain among us and our sons and daughters." Glancing around the room at the dearth of people thirty-five and under—the age I was then and that many of the second generation would have also been—made that obvious. If the Mosque of Islamic Brotherhood could not survive among us, what hope did it and its values have within a third generation? If those problems are unresolved and that pain still unhealed among people like Talib's and my father's grandchildren, what hope should any movement and the values it espouses have for the future?

In researching the Banu (or Bani) Hilal tribe, the Bedouin sons of the crescent moon for whom Imam Tawfiq nicknamed his congregation, I learned that it disappeared tragically in the eleventh century following a defeat in battle. The tribe, as it was known, simply ceased to exist. Small groups and individuals who survived, however, dispersed all over North Africa, taking tales of their tribal history and poems of their dramatic exploits with them. Epic poems about the Banu Hilal could be heard from Morocco to Iraq and even in Spain some two hundred years after the tribe's defeat, all the way up to the nineteenth century. The verses were called upon especially during times of crisis, used as a means to unite and inspire. Historians say that had the tribe continued to thrive, though, its poetry and history would likely never have permeated the Arab world. Tales about the Banu Hilal would have stayed within the Banu Hilal, robbing the region of a great oral tradition and wonderful stories of legendary conquests. It's only now, as storytellers who still recite the poetry in Egypt are dying out and no one is stepping up to continue the tradition, that the legend of the Banu Hilal is in danger.

That's how I think of Tawfiq's Banu-Hilal—his Mosque of Islamic Brotherhood. Over the years, there have been many dispersals of members, for whatever reason. Each person who leaves carries with him or her tales of exploits as a son or daughter of the crescent moon and passes them on to his or her own children. They are stories of hopefulness, idealism, impulsiveness, naïveté, faith, passion, and love. They are stories of a time and of a people. No one's story is the same. But those stories my father and mother told me about the great spirit of hope that inspired them to become Muslim and all the striving my father in particular did with MIB to realize a dream—that's the legacy I inherited. Although his efforts weren't successful, it is a proud legacy.

When I was growing up, I didn't understand it. All I had was the dream deferred. After looking back, both with my parents and on my own, I now not only understand it, but with its imperfections, scars, and blisters intact, I accept it. In spite of itself, the legacy of that dream lives on.

It is nighttime, and I am trying to get Samaadi to settle into the hush of the hour. At a year and a half old, he is all energy, running everywhere as if walking doesn't exist, giggling with no air so hysterically it's contagious to anyone within earshot; his dusty black hair always springing, his chubby round stomach always growling, his slender brown fingers always pressing. He grabs onto my comforter and climbs up to my bed so I can read him bedtime stories. They won't calm him for sleep, but he listens and turns the pages. After we shut the last one, I tell him, "OK. It's time to pray."

I close my eyes, bow my head, and part my hands cupped before my face. I reach over and position Samaadi to do the same. Returning to my posture, I begin to sing the Arabic words I learned as a girl seated on the living room couch with my family surrounding me those nights so long ago.

"*Bismillah al-rahman al-rahim,*" I start slowly so Samaadi can make out what I'm saying.

"*Alhamdulillahi rabbi-il al-amin.*"

He stretches his body out atop my purple, leaf-printed comforter and touches the books, clearly more interesting than whatever he thinks it is that I'm doing. I continue: "*Al-rahman al-rahim. Maliki yawmi din. Iyyaka na-buduwa, iyyaka nasta'iyn.*"

Samaadi glances up at me, then slides himself feet first off of the bed. He begins to bounce around, over to the closet, across to my small iron bookcase, and back to the bed. He wants to get up again. I reach down and help lift the little busybody beside me.

"*Ikhdinas siraa-til mustaqim.*"

Samaadi is quiet for a while, and I lower my eyes, focusing on the words of the prayer that has never left me. Their utterance, this reverential act of worship, has always brought me near to Allah—even when far from friends, schoolmates, and my family—drawn close, like each other's keeper. This is what I share with my son.

"*Siraa-til ikhdina 'an 'amta 'allayhim. Guyril makdubi 'allayhim.*" When I reach the end and close the prayer, saying, "*Walla-dau leen. Amin,*" Samaadi grasps his little palms beneath my knuckles and pushes my fingers up to my face. He has been paying attention. A grin spreads across his lips as our clasped hands, together, wash God's blessings first over me and then over him. We are cleansed.

I know my son has no idea what I said as we prayed. He doesn't yet know the point of making a prayer or maybe even what a prayer is. It will take some time for him to understand why we do what we do. But I am reassured by the thought that one day, he will know.

REFERENCES

The following articles, books, and recordings were critical to the writing of this book.

Abdullah, A. Rashid. "Islam and Nationalism: The Politics of Independence." *Western Sunrise* (New York), May 1972, 4–13.

Abdur-Rahman, Hasan I. Letter. *Western Sunrise* (New York), August 1973, 14.

Associated Negro Press. "Abyssinian Church, N.Y. Quits National Council." *Indianapolis Recorder*, April 5, 1952, 9.

Barrett, Paul M. *American Islam: The Struggle for the Soul of a Religion.* New York: Picador, 2007.

Bethune-Cookman University. *The B-Cean, 1969.* Electronic reproduction, University of Central Florida Libraries, 2009.

———. *The B-Cean, 1970.* Electronic reproduction, University of Central Florida Libraries, 2009.

Breitman, George, ed. *Malcolm X Speaks: Selected Speeches and Statements.* 1965. New York: Grove Weidenfeld, 1990.

Dannin, Robert. *Black Pilgrimage to Islam.* New York: Oxford University Press, 2002.

Davis, Thulani. *Malcolm X: The Great Photographs.* Edited by Howard Chapnick. New York: Stewart, Tabori & Chang, 1993.

Doyle, Patrick, Thomas Raftery, and Harry Stathos. "4 Slain in B'klyn Muslim Gun Battle: 3 Surviving Raiders at Mosque Escape; 1 Badly Wounded." *Daily News*, February 5, 1974, 1, 3, 56.

"Epic Tales of Arab Bravery." *Al Jazeera*, November 17, 2003. https://www.aljazeera.com/news/2003/11/17/epic-tales-of-arab-bravery.

Gendar, Alison. "Nation of Islam Mosque Killing of NYPD Cop Still a Mystery, 37 Years Later." *Daily News*, March 21, 2009. www.nydailynews.com/news/crime/nation-islam-mosque-killing-nypd-mystery-37-years-article-1.369007.

Goodman, George, Jr. "Man Held for Robbery Indicted in Slaying of Priest." *New York Times*, June 28, 1973. https://www.nytimes.com/1973/06/28/archives /man-held-for-robbery-indicted-in-slaying-of-priest-collection-money.html.

Honko, Lauri, ed. *Textualization of Oral Epics*. New York: De Gruyter Mouton, 2000.

Ibrahim, Mahmoud Andrade. *The Dar Ul Islam Movement: An American Odyssey Revisited*. CreateSpace, 2010.

Kirkman, Edward. "Muslim Shootout Puts Cops on Alert." *Daily News* (New York), February 6, 1974, 34.

Levitt, Leonard. "Remembering Cardillo and the Mosque." *One Police Plaza*, April 13, 2009. http://206.188.4.211/columns/2009/090413.html.

Lincoln, C. Eric. "The Power in the Black Church." *Cross Currents* 24, no. 1 (1974): 3–21.

McQuiston, John T. "4 Die in Brooklyn Mosque in Shootout by 2 Factions." *New York Times*, February 5, 1974, 1, 73.

Morrison, Micah. "Did an FBI Call Accidentally Kill an NYPD Officer?" *New York Post*, April 19, 2015. nypost.com/2015/04/19/did-an-fbi-call-accidentally -kill-an-nypd-officer/.

Muhammad, Abdur Rahman. "Imam Talib Abdur-Rasheed [sic] Responds." *A Singular Voice*, January 9, 2008. Copy in possession of author.

———."Why Blackamerican Muslims Don't Stand for Justice. Pt. 2." *A Singular Voice*, November 22, 2007. Copy in possession of author.

"Name Negro VP of National Maritime Union." *Jet*, May 14, 1959, 3.

Pace, Eric. "5 Policemen Hurt in Harlem Melee." *New York Times*, April 15, 1972, 1.

Reynolds, Dwight Fletcher. *Heroic Poets, Poetic Heroes: The Ethnography of Performance in an Arabic Oral Epic Tradition*. Ithaca, NY: Cornell University Press, 1995.

Sheppard, Nathaniel, Jr. "Police Search for 3 Men in Mosque Slayings Here." *New York Times*, February 6, 1974, 44.

Tawfiq, K. Ahmad. "Clarity of Intention." Khutbah at Mosque of Islamic Brotherhood, New York, March 14, 1980. Recording in possession of author.

———. "WomanHood." Khutbah at Mosque of Islamic Brotherhood, New York, September 25, 1981. Recording in possession of author.

Turner, Richard Brent. *Islam in the African-American Experience*. 2nd ed. Bloomington: Indiana University Press, 2003.

Western Sunrise (New York), 1971–1974.

Wofford, Susanne Lindgren. *Epic Traditions in the Contemporary World: The Poetics of Community.* Berkeley: University of California Press, 1999.

X, Malcolm. "The Black Revolution." In *Malcolm X Speaks: Selected Speeches and Statements,* edited by George Breitman, 45–57. 1965. New York: Grove Weidenfeld, 1990.

———. "White Man's Law." In *Malcolm X: The Best of the Speeches.* Stardust Records, 2007. music.apple.com/us/album/the-best-of-the-speeches /261688246.

ACKNOWLEDGMENTS

Alhamdulillahi rabbi-il al-amin. Praise be to Allah, Lord of the Worlds. I thank God for giving me the strength, perseverance, and sense of purpose to complete this book and bring it to the world.

I am eternally grateful to the people who were patient and forthcoming as I interviewed them, even before I knew what the story was, including: Abi, Ummi, Abdullah Abdur-Razzaq, Baha Oudin Abdul-Malik, Kwami Taha, A. Rashid Abdullah, Mustafa Abdul-Azim, Abdur-Rahman Zaid, Khadija Abdul-Karim, Khalil Abdul-Karim, Zahiyya Abdul-Karim, Abdul-Qawiy Abdul-Karim, Juwariya Abdul-Quddus, Nadia Abdul-Quddus, Najwa Aisha Comeau, Jibril Abdus-Samad, Luqman Abdush-Shahid, Imam Talib Abdur-Rashid, Halima Toure, Abdul-Malik Muhammad, Gregory Nimmo, Janice Carroll, Robin Nesbitt, and all members of my mother's sisterhood.

This book also benefits from the work of others who came before and helped put my thinking into context, which includes: *The Autobiography of Malcolm X* as told to Alex Haley (One World, 1964); *Growing Up X* by Ilyasah Shabazz with Kim McLarin (One World, 2002); *Little X: Growing Up in the Nation of Islam* by Sonsyrea Tate (University of Tennessee Press, 2005); *Muslim Cool: Race, Religion, and Hip Hop in the United States* by Su'ad Abdul Khabeer (NYU Press, 2016); *The Black Power Movement: Rethinking the Civil Rights-Black Power Era*, edited by Peniel E. Joseph (Routledge, 2006); and *Waiting 'Til the Midnight Hour: A Narrative History of Black Power in America* by Peniel E. Joseph (Holt, 2006).

To my parents, my sincerest thanks for your support, in whatever form that may take in any given moment. I thank you also for giving me five amazing siblings with whom I can share joys and pains and our particular brand of crazy. Idris, I love you. Aqil, you're an inspiration. Aliya, thanks for always having my back. Isa, I owe you. Moe, you're a light.

I'm fortunate to have had the encouragement of a number of writing communities while I've worked on this book. Thanks to the faculty and graduates of Goucher College's MFA in Creative Nonfiction Program, including Patsy Sims, Leslie Rubinkowski, Laura Wexler, Jacob Levenson, Suzannah Lessard, Diana

Hume George, Theo Emery, and Jesse J. Holland. Thanks to the organizers, the faculty, and my classmates at the VONA/Voices Workshop. I appreciate you, Faith Adiele, Reyna Grande, Carmen Inguanzo, Itzel Basualdo, Mariela Regalado, Jocelyn Duffy, Ana Maria Owusu-Tyo, Jenny Tinghui Zhang, Jesus Iniguez Rivas, Jani White, Yesenia Flores Diaz, and, especially, my crew, Nicky Andrews, Shizue Seigel, Billy Gong, Nathaniel Carter, Debra Rivera, Kendra Collins, Rosanna Salcedo, and Jessica Yen. Thanks to the wonderful people at the Residency at Mineral School: Jane Hodges, Elizabeth Eaves, and my fellow residents, Kelly Morse, Marjorie Celona, and Emily Tuszynska.

I'm grateful for my talented colleagues at Washington College, Sean Meehan, James Allen Hall, Roy Kesey, Kimberly Quiogue Andrews, Elizabeth O'Connor, Rich De Prospo, Courtney Rydel, Katie Charles, Alisha Knight, and those at Bowie State University, David Basena, David Kaloustian, Nicole Wilson, Tanya McInnis, Yao Glover, Monifa Asante Love, Jenise Williamson, Horacio Sierra, Shelagh Johnson, Chris Murray, many others, and the students of both institutions who challenged me and cheered me on.

I'm forever indebted to the greatest training ground in the world, Howard University, and my classmates and instructors, namely Lawrence Jackson and Lawrence Kaggwa.

I'm thankful for friends who've never stopped believing in me: Mary Koles, Elena Rushing, Keith Rushing, Magin LaSov Gregg, Mike Scalise, Susan Land, Dannette Hutchinson, and Sonya Ephraim.

I thank the students of the Iowa Writers' Workshop for all the work they did to push my book forward in the Prize for Literary Nonfiction and a huge thank you to judge Susan Steinberg for selecting it. I thank the staff of the University of Iowa Press for being patient with me.

Thanks, also, to Dustin Craun of *Ummah Wide* for first publishing "Surrender at the Cinema."

Thank you to the rest of my family, Nigel and Monica Scott, Duane, Tracy, Omar, Tara, and Brian Maitland, for picking up the slack whenever I needed help. Thank you, Kenneth Taylor, for your vision, and Wade Taylor Jr., for your encouragement.

Endless hugs and kisses go to my loves, my boys, Samaadi and Madiba, brilliant both. Heartfelt gratitude goes to my husband, Rion Amilcar Scott, for your inspiration, guidance, and for always making me see the impossible as possible.

Lastly, I'd like to acknowledge the memory of my grandfather, Wade H. Taylor Sr. Poppi, your stories inspired me from the start; I'm honored to continue the tradition of storytelling about our family.

IOWA PRIZE FOR LITERARY NONFICTION

Heir to the Crescent Moon
by Sufiya Abdur-Rahman

When You Learn the Alphabet
by Kendra Allen

*China Lake: A Journey into the Contradicted
Heart of a Global Climate Catastrophe*
by Barret Baumgart

Faculty Brat: A Memoir of Abuse
by Dominic Bucca

*Kissing Fidel: A Memoir of Cuban-American
Terrorism in the United States*
by Magda Montiel Davis

For Single Mothers Working as Train Conductors
by Laura Esther Wolfson